AUSTRALIA

THE PHOTOGRAPHER'S VIEW

AUSTRALIA

THE PHOTOGRAPHER'S VIEW

From the 1850s to the Bicentenary

Robert Coupe

Longman Cheshire Pty Limited
Longman House
Kings Gardens
95 Coventry Street
Melbourne 3205 Australia

Offices in Sydney, Brisbane, Adelaide
and Perth. Associated companies, branches,
and representatives throughout the world.

First published 1987

Designed by R. T. J. Klinkhamer
Set in New Century (condensed 2 points) by Dead Set Pty Ltd, Melbourne
Produced by Longman Cheshire Pty Ltd
Printed in Hong Kong

National Library of Australia
Cataloguing-in-Publication data

Coupe, Robert.
Australia, the photographer's view.
ISBN 0 582 66357 1.
1. Australia — History. 2. Australia — History —
Pictorial works. I. Title.
994'.0022'2

Contents

Introduction

The first photograph was made in France in the mid-1820s by Joseph Nicéphore Niépce, who later collaborated with Louis Daguerre to develop the process known as *daguerreotype* — a photographic image produced by the action of light on a chemically treated silver surface. In Australia the daguerreotype photographers, involved mainly in portraiture, were active in the 1840s and by the middle of the century there were about fifty photographic studios established in the main cities of the eastern colonies, as well as a number of travelling photographers. But the system was clumsy and the results, at least by modern standards, left much to be desired.

Wet-plate photography — pioneered by Abel Niépce de St Victor, a cousin of the earlier Niépce — by which the exposure time could be reduced to as little as five seconds, arrived in Australia in the mid-1850s and greatly increased the range of subjects and locations that could be captured photographically, as well as making it possible for an indefinite number of prints to be printed from a single glass negative. Photographers such as Fauchery and Merlin used wet-plate photography to produce some of the finest Australian documentary photographs of the goldrush era. The development of dry-plate photography in the 1880s and its subsequent refinement into the now familiar roll of film was the work of the American who introduced the Kodak camera in 1888, George Eastman. The result was liberating, putting the camera into the hands of thousands of amateur enthusiasts, who recorded, with varying degrees of expertise, almost every aspect of the public life of the emerging nation.

This book presents scenes from almost 140 years of Australian history as recorded by a large number of amateur and professional photographers. The photographs range from carefully posed and often stilted portraits of individuals and groups, to spontaneous shots of domestic and public scenes. They reflect the capacity of the camera to capture the immediacy of events, and the ways in which it has been exploited to produce calculated effects or promote desired images.

Prospector's Hut
LINDT, Photo

1
The Victorian Era
1850 – 1900

HAVELOCK
Tobacco

By 1850 many of the features that were to determine the shape of Australian society had already emerged and patterns for future development were clearly discernible. The transportation of law-breakers, the basis on which the society was built, had almost ended — only Western Australia was still receiving convicts, and in eastern Australia Port Arthur alone remained as an ignominious vestige of the convict era. The major cities now existed and were growing, and the pattern of predominantly coastal habitation had been established. The great pastoral industries were set to expand, and sheep and (to a lesser extent) wheat were the economic mainstays of colonial society. Exploration and settlement had more or less defined the extent of possible habitation and the nature of development in the habitable areas. Aboriginal society had been subjugated to the will and convenience of the newcomers and an almost entirely homogeneous white population predominated.

The discovery of gold in the 1850s unleashed forces that were to transform the existing society. The influx of treasure-seekers that continued until the end of the century greatly swelled the population, created new towns and industries and gave rise to the enduring Australian myth, exemplified at the Eureka Stockade, of rugged self-reliance and distrust of constituted authority. The arrival of large numbers of Chinese, posing a threat to racial homogeneity, confirmed, too, a racist tendency in Australian society that would be enshrined in the 'White Australia' provisions of the Constitution.

Exploration in the later nineteenth century concentrated on the arid inland. It established beyond doubt the inhospitable nature, at least from an Anglo-European viewpoint, of the continent's centre, and finally laid to rest such fanciful but persistent notions as the existence of an inland sea.

Self-government came to the colonies between 1846 and 1891, and a desire for nationhood gradually took hold. After much bitter wrangling and the reluctant abandonment of some parochial interests, federation was eventually achieved — symbolically as one century gave way to another, and almost simultaneously with the passing of Queen Victoria, the living symbol of the age.

Previous pages: A group of prospectors, carefully posed but affecting nonchalance, examine their finds in front of a crude bush hut near Solferino in the central west of New South Wales. Gold was discovered in the region in the early 1870s.

Left: 'Down on his Luck', one of a series of studies depicting aspects of pioneering life in Gippsland in the 1870s by Nicholas Caire (1837-1918). This settler has set up and equipped his home in the burnt-out hollow of a giant gum.

Entitled 'Gippsland Scenery', this study by Caire, with its delicately diffused sunlight and the seemingly relaxed manner of the men and animals, presents a rather idealised impression of a selector's life in Victoria's Gippsland area.

To Europeans the Australian Aborigines were a primitive and exotic race. Although their complex cultural traditions and nomadic lifestyle were neither understood nor valued, Aborigines were regarded, especially from afar, as quaintly picturesque. This attitude is reflected in these highly romanticised portraits, with their carefully contrived and meticulously composed backgrounds, by Antoine Fauchery. Fauchery came to Australia in 1857, commissioned by the French government to document, both in photographs and sketches, aspects of Australian life. The Aboriginal people of Gippsland were the subjects of many of his works. In the bottom photograph particularly, the Aboriginal men, cloaked in possum skins and with shields, boomerangs and spears displayed for maximum visual effect, look every bit the European ideal of the noble savage. The top photograph, with its domestic theme, more accurately depicts the nature of Aboriginal experience in a colonial setting. The ceremonial scarring on the woman's body and the metal cooking utensils are indicative of the mingling of Aboriginal and European cultures that was apparent by the later nineteenth century.

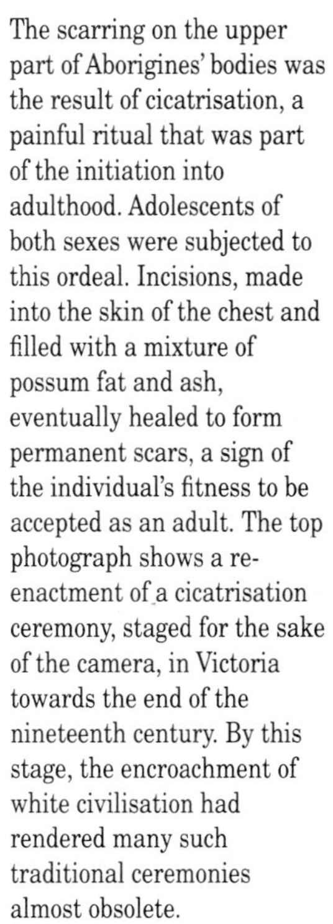

The scarring on the upper part of Aborigines' bodies was the result of cicatrisation, a painful ritual that was part of the initiation into adulthood. Adolescents of both sexes were subjected to this ordeal. Incisions, made into the skin of the chest and filled with a mixture of possum fat and ash, eventually healed to form permanent scars, a sign of the individual's fitness to be accepted as an adult. The top photograph shows a re-enactment of a cicatrisation ceremony, staged for the sake of the camera, in Victoria towards the end of the nineteenth century. By this stage, the encroachment of white civilisation had rendered many such traditional ceremonies almost obsolete.

As white settlement spread and as squatters occupied large tracts of hitherto virgin land, inevitable and often bloody confrontations occurred betweeen the newcomers and the Aborigines they displaced. Attacks by Aborigines on sheep and property frequently resulted in brutal and indiscriminate reprisals. In the bottom picture the paternalistic gesture that Angus McMillan, a squatter in Gippsland in the 1840s and 1850s, is making towards the cowed-looking Aborigines is somewhat at odds with the fact that in 1840 he had established his right to a piece of territory by organising the killing of all the Aborigines that could be found in the area and was the leader of at least one other retributive massacre. A staunch upholder of the Christian faith, McMillan boasted of his humanitarian attitudes towards those blacks who had been spared his wrath.

Although both agriculture and permanent settlement conflicted with the traditions of Aboriginal tribal life, by the second half of the nineteenth century many of those who had survived the ravages of massacres and introduced diseases had made the necessary accommodations to white values. As pastoral stations grew and prospered Aborigines represented for whites a ready source of cheap labour as well as an opportunity to play a civilising and proselytising role. Although destined to remain on the periphery of white society, some Aborigines, like this farming family at Cooranderrk station in Victoria, had adopted at least the trappings of European society.

In many communities cordial and even affectionate relations developed between the Aboriginal and white communities. From 1890, William Henry Corkhill, an amateur photographic enthusiast, recorded many aspects of life in the small settlement of Tilba Tilba in southern New South Wales. This picture shows whites and obviously assimilated Aborigines at the funeral of 'Queen' Narelle of the Wallaga Lake tribe. The photograph, although carefully posed, does suggest an easy and natural mingling of white and black communities and a genuine respect among the white mourners for the memory of the old Aboriginal who for many years had been a prominent local identity.

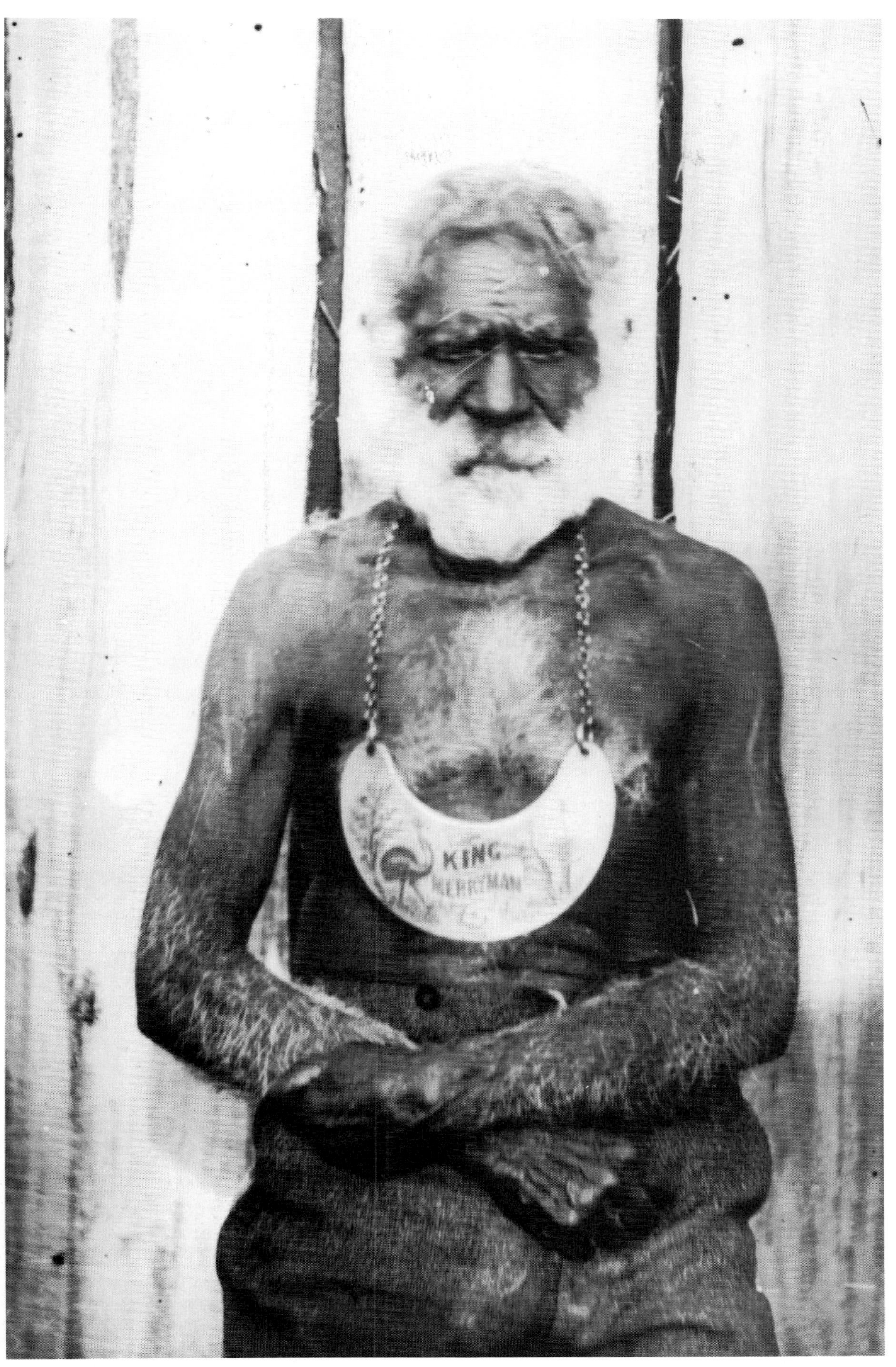

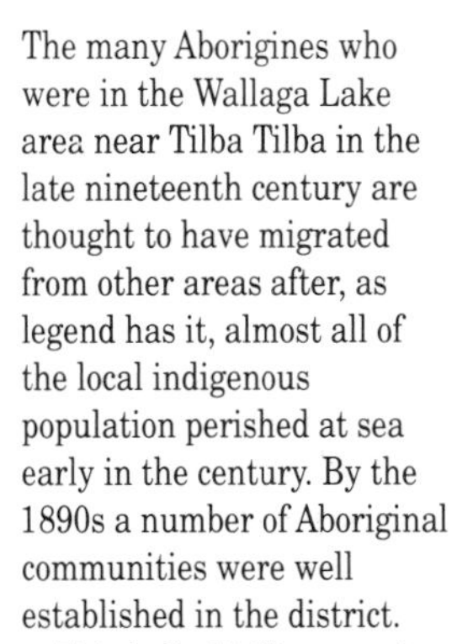

The many Aborigines who were in the Wallaga Lake area near Tilba Tilba in the late nineteenth century are thought to have migrated from other areas after, as legend has it, almost all of the local indigenous population perished at sea early in the century. By the 1890s a number of Aboriginal communities were well established in the district.

This is Corkhill's portrait of 'King' Merriman, the husband of 'Queen' Narelle and the last of the district's tribal elders. A rather pathetic looking figure, he is wearing the demeaning 'king plate' (complete with a misspelling of his name), a symbol both of his status in the Aboriginal community and of the condescension with which even well-intentioned whites regarded that community. In contrast to the proud nobility of bearing that tribal Aborigines displayed in many earlier portraits, this tribal elder's hunched shoulders, sagging physique and elusive gaze, as well as the graceless trousers that have been imposed upon him in the cause of decent dress, seem to express the demoralised state to which half-Europeanised remnants of Aboriginal tribes had been reduced.

A study by Antoine Fauchery of a group panning for gold at Castlemaine in Victoria in 1857. Gold was discovered in Castlemaine in 1851 and by 1857 some 31 000 miners had flocked to the goldfield there, known originally as Forest Creek and then Mount Alexander. The rich alluvial finds of the region became legendary but eventually the surface gold petered out and large-scale reef mining took over from the individual efforts of men like these.

Diggers assemble at a protest meeting at the Ivanhoe Venture in Western Australia in 1898. By this time the easily won alluvial finds near the surface had been worked out and mining was becoming a big business in the hands of companies who employed miners on wages. Those who had come to the goldfield in the expectation of making a fortune by their own skills or good luck were disillusioned by the prospect of working as labourers with nothing more than a weekly wage as their reward.

Antoine Fauchery, the French photographer and artist, arrived providentially in Victoria as the goldrushes were gaining momentum. He went to the Victorian goldfields and became a chronicler, in his letters as well as in his photographs, of the goldrush era. He was also a successful digger. This photo shows a group of immigrants from Cornwall pretending, not very convincingly, that they have been caught unearthing the 'Welcome Stranger' nugget, the largest single nugget ever discovered in Australia. It weighed almost 80 000 grams and was discovered at Moliagul in central Victoria when the wheel of a dray fortuitously exposed it to view.

The 'Welcome Stranger' nugget was not discovered until 1869 when the rush of diggers to the Victorian goldfields had dramatically declined after the heady days of the 1850s. Earlier spectacular and widely publicised finds, such as that of the only slightly smaller 'Welcome' nugget in 1858, had helped fuel the gold fever that sent thousands of people flocking in search of a quick and, in most cases, an elusive fortune.

North of Bathurst in New South Wales is the now almost deserted town of Hill End which, during the early 1870s, was a thriving goldrush town with 8000 inhabitants, who were served by five banks and two newspapers. Like the nearby gold town of Gulgong, Hill End was exhaustively documented in Beaufoy Merlin's wet-plate photographs. Almost every building was photographed individually and the collection, now housed in the Mitchell Library, Sydney, is an unsurpassed and authentic record of a boom town at its height. The four photographs on these two pages are all by Merlin.

The top photograph shows the main street of Hill End in about 1871. Although most of the shops — many of them crude and makeshift structures — had been built by that time, the unsealed roads and footpaths were, depending on the weather, either quagmires or dustbowls. The sturdy two-storey brick building at the far end on the right is the Royal Hotel. It is now the only survivor of the 28 inns and hostelries that serviced the town at the height of the goldrush.

Coleman's store (*bottom*) is typical of many commercial enterprises in the goldrush towns, both in its ramshackle construction and in the jumbled variety of goods it offered for sale. Also typical is the conspicuous timber hoarding that boldly proclaims the enterprise. In 1872 Hill End contained more than a kilometre of shops and other commercial premises. Few of these hastily constructed buildings survive.

Whereas much of Hill End remains as a vestigial reminder of the goldrush days and even contains many relics of the era housed in a museum, other smaller towns that sprang up in the central west of New South Wales proved more ephemeral. One of these was Home Rule whose almost deserted main street was captured in this atmospheric photograph by Beaufoy Merlin. The tree stumps and the number of as yet unfelled trees in the street show that the town was still in an early stage of development. It was to grow into a bustling little town that could sustain two hotels, a billiard saloon and a post office.

The more substantial and still thriving town of Gulgong, not far from Hill End, was the scene of a late goldrush. Gold was first discovered in the vicinity in 1870 and the 'village of Gulgong' was gazetted in 1872. It quickly grew into a sizeable community with a range of stores, some of them with such outlandish names as 'The Greatest Wonder of the World', and a theatre — the Prince of Wales — which attracted some of the best available acting and musical talent to its stage. The presence of Merlin and his camera in the town in about 1872 obviously brought quite a collection of shopkeepers and other locals, as well as two curious dogs, out into the main street.

By the late 1870s alluvial mining and small claims had to a great extent given way to larger-scale enterprises involving mechanisation and considerable capital outlay as shafts were sunk to exploit reefs deep below the surface. This photograph of the Victorian mountain settlement of Blackwood, taken by Nicholas Caire in about 1877, shows the degree to which these developments could transform a township and further contribute to the destruction of the natural environment. In the background, dominating the town both visually and no doubt by the din it produced, stands the steam-powered battery where the quartz that was extracted from the earth was crushed. The denuded timber-strewn landscape and the piles of dirt enhance the general feeling of desolation.

The priorities of goldmining communities can be gauged from this picture of the main street of the small Victorian town of Mount William. Prominent among the commercial enterprises that have established substantial premises are the Cosmopolitan Hotel and James Dunphy's wine and spirit store, while the miners are still housed in tents.

In 1851 John Dunlop and Thomas Regan happened on gold in the area that is now the handsome and thriving agricultural town of Ballarat in central Victoria. Before the end of the year almost 10 000 hopeful treasure-seekers had flocked to the region and were frantically scouring the earth. By the end of the decade this population had more than doubled and Ballarat was easily the largest of Victoria's inland towns.

In 1860, the laying of the foundation stone for the imposing stone town hall, one of the fine Victorian buildings that still adorn the city, was an important event that occasioned a gathering of dignitaries and representatives of many civic groups, including the Ballarat Fire Brigade whose banner dominates the centre of this photograph. This was still the era of alluvial mining and most of the town's population lived in what is now East Ballarat, either in timber cottages such as those that are visible in the background or in makeshift canvas structures.

Gold was not discovered in Western Australia until the early 1890s. The discoveries were fortuitous; while the eastern colonies languished under the effects of a major depression, the West enjoyed a period of boom as thousands rushed there in search of the precious metal. Areas in the Pilbara and Kimberley regions were opened up for settlement by Europeans and in the south the towns of Coolgardie and Kalgoorlie were established.

The West Australian goldfields were in remote desert areas where lack of water created serious problems. As much of the prospecting was done in dry earth, the traditional cradle or sluice box could not be used to sift out the gold. Dry-blowing techniques, which made use of the wind, were used instead. Behind the miners in this picture is a specially developed machine — a 'Wood's dry placer miner' — that used bellows instead of wind to separate the finer soil and dust as it fell through a series of sieves. The bellows were driven by a belt which was operated by turning the small hand-wheel on the left.

The gold towns that had grown up forty years earlier in the east were prototypes for the West Australian gold towns of the nineties as this picture of Bailey Street Coolgardie, taken in 1894, clearly shows. The flat desert landscape, sparse in vegetation and lacking in contours, imposed few restrictions on space and allowed for streets of enormous width.

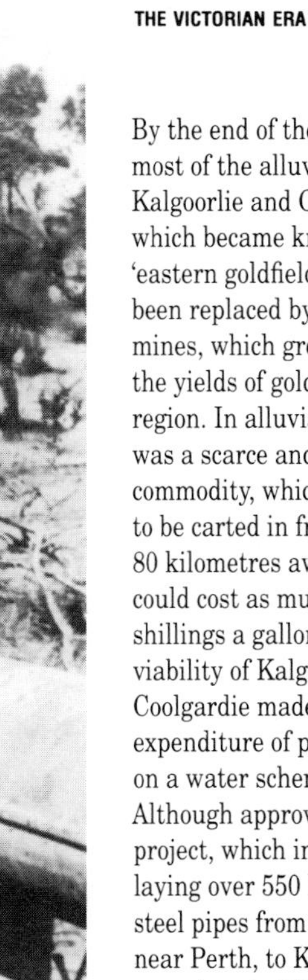

By the end of the century most of the alluvial mining in Kalgoorlie and Coolgardie — which became known as the 'eastern goldfields' — had been replaced by deep shaft mines, which greatly boosted the yields of gold from the region. In alluvial days water was a scarce and precious commodity, which often had to be carted in from as far as 80 kilometres away and could cost as much as two shillings a gallon. The proven viability of Kalgoorlie and Coolgardie made the expenditure of public funds on a water scheme feasible. Although approval for the project, which involved laying over 550 kilometres of steel pipes from Mundaring, near Perth, to Kalgoorlie, was given in 1895, the water did not begin to flow until 1903.

South Australia was the only colony where payable gold was not discovered and which did not experience a genuine rush. A number of finds were made, however, notably at Tarcoola and Teetulpa, and these attracted some prospectors in the 1870s. At Teetulpa a sprawling city of tents and crudely constructed brush shelters grew up and the nutritional needs of the miners were catered for, at least in part, by a 'pie man', posing here with his produce precariously balanced.

Until the advent and eventual expansion of the railway system horses provided the only means of transportation for the vast majority of Australians and until well into the twentieth century horse-drawn vehicles were the principal form of road transport. The seven horses that came to this country with the First Fleet in 1788 grew in number in the next 130 years to more than two and a half million. During the nineteenth century the horse was indispensable.

For dwellers in remote areas smaller horse-drawn vehicles, such as the one in the centre picture, provided their only link with centres of population; people who travelled between cities or towns rode in more commodious vehicles like the Royal Mail coach (*top*), which is collecting and setting down mail in the Victorian town of Queenstown. As well as passengers and mail these coaches also carried goods. Along the main coaching routes a large number of inns grew up to serve the needs of the coach travellers and to stable, feed and water the horses.

In 1871, when the bottom picture was taken, horse-drawn road transport was still the principal means of transporting rural produce, even though a network of railways had been established. Here, cartloads of wool are arriving at the lower end of Macquarie Street, Sydney, to be stored in warehouses before being loaded onto clipper ships for export.

In the 1850s an enterprising American, Freeman Cobb, and three compatriots established Cobb & Co, a new coaching firm, and imported lightweight American 'jack' coaches that were well suited to the rough conditions of local roads and tracks. The coaches' bodies were suspended on leather straps, which were attached to the undercarriage by curved metal pieces called 'jacks'. In the 1860s another American, James Rutherford of Bathurst, took over the company and greatly expanded its operation. Coaches, based on the American models, were manufactured locally and within a decade the name Cobb & Co became synonymous with long-distance travel in the eastern colonies. The Nicholas Caire photograph (*top*) shows a Cobb & Co coach taking a group of Aborigines to the Lake Tyers Aboriginal reserve east of Lakes Entrance in Victoria. The driver is being handed a small leather satchel known as a 'waybill pouch' which was attached to the iron rail on his right.

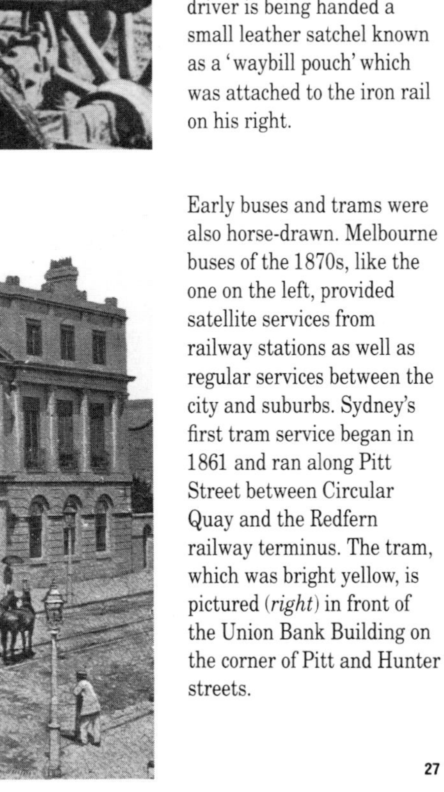

Early buses and trams were also horse-drawn. Melbourne buses of the 1870s, like the one on the left, provided satellite services from railway stations as well as regular services between the city and suburbs. Sydney's first tram service began in 1861 and ran along Pitt Street between Circular Quay and the Redfern railway terminus. The tram, which was bright yellow, is pictured (*right*) in front of the Union Bank Building on the corner of Pitt and Hunter streets.

Despite their obvious suitability for the barren expanses of the Australian outback, and their superiority to horses for many tasks, camels were too exotic a species to be accepted easily by a population that was predominantly of British stock and that clung tenaciously to British traditions and ways, even when these conflicted with climatic and other environmental imperatives. The importation of camels was a piecemeal business that began tentatively in the 1840s but did not catch on seriously until 1860 when 24 camels were brought into Victoria from India for the Burke and Wills expedition. Thereafter their usefulness became obvious and they played a valuable role in the building of the Overland Telegraph and in many exploratory expeditions. By the end of the century there were about 6000 camels in Australia and two-thirds of these were in Western Australia, with significant numbers in South Australia and western New South Wales.

Their genuine usefulness is somewhat belied by photographs such as the one (*top*) in which an elegantly attired woman looks decidedly incongruous atop a beast she would probably never have mounted except for the presence of a camera. The other photograph (*bottom*), taken in 1894, provides a better example of the practical use of camels.

Towards the end of the nineteenth century the bicycle, probably more than any other form of transport, offered the chance of independent mobility to individual Australians. Bicycles first came to Australia in the 1860s, but their 'penny-farthing' construction and solid rubber tyres made them hazardous and difficult to manoeuvre for any but the committed enthusiast. The members of the South Australian Bicycle Club (*top*), pictured here in the late 1870s against a background designed to suggest the pleasures of country cycling, probably did not venture too far afield on their clumsy-looking machines.

By the 1880s the modern bicycle had evolved, with the development of tubular steel frames, inflatable tyres and chain drive. By the end of the century mass production had made cycling a popular pastime as well as a practical mode of transport. Cycling clubs abounded in both rural and urban areas.

An enthusiasm for cycling even encouraged some more daring women to forsake their voluminous skirts in favour of trousers or 'slacks'. One such stands in the middle of this otherwise thoroughly decorous group of young lady enthusiasts, posing demurely beside a suburban fence in Adelaide, and seemingly unaware of the furtive observer behind them. A lone male at the back of the group acts as escort. The covering over the rear wheel of the bicycle on the left helped prevent the embarrassing and possibly dangerous consequences of skirts becoming entangled in the spokes.

Steam was the great driving force of the nineteenth century; it revolutionised both transportation and industry. River steamers provided a vital link between the many settlements that grew up along the rivers all around the continent and in Tasmania, and especially on the extensive Murray-Darling system. Throughout the second half of the nineteenth century and in the first decade of the twentieth, paddle steamers such as this plied the Murray, Darling and Murrumbidgee rivers, transporting passengers and goods, promoting trade, and opening up previously inaccessible areas for settlement and development. The spread of rail systems gradually supplanted the steamers and from the 1880s river transport declined.

Although the motor car was one of the great novelties of the new century, and would not be widely accessible until the 1920s, some steam-driven precursors of the private car were occasionally to be seen in the late 1890s. This rather ungainly looking model, powered by a wood-fired water boiler, was built by David Shearer, a South Australian maker of farm machinery, in 1897. He is seen here taking his family for a drive. With all aboard the car could reach a top speed of 24 kilometres an hour.

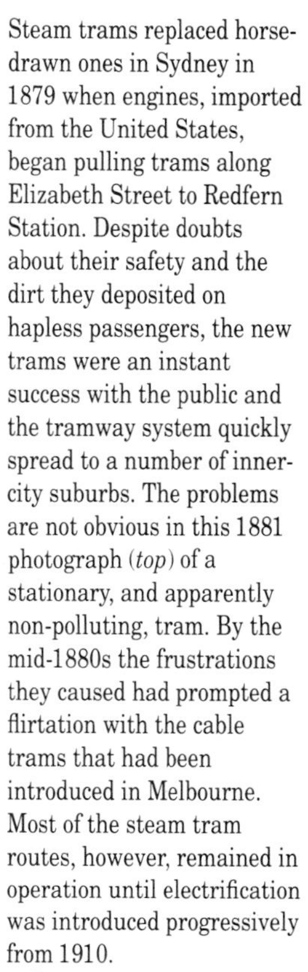
Steam trams replaced horse-drawn ones in Sydney in 1879 when engines, imported from the United States, began pulling trams along Elizabeth Street to Redfern Station. Despite doubts about their safety and the dirt they deposited on hapless passengers, the new trams were an instant success with the public and the tramway system quickly spread to a number of inner-city suburbs. The problems are not obvious in this 1881 photograph (*top*) of a stationary, and apparently non-polluting, tram. By the mid-1880s the frustrations they caused had prompted a flirtation with the cable trams that had been introduced in Melbourne. Most of the steam tram routes, however, remained in operation until electrification was introduced progressively from 1910.

Steam trains in Australia got off to an inauspicious start. The first line to operate, in Victoria, covered a distance of a mere 4 kilometres from the docks at Port Melbourne to a platform in Flinders Street. The locomotive that pulled the train proved unequal to the task and had to be replaced after five days by a truck with a piledriver mounted on it. The steam locomotive (*bottom*) was, despite its name, not the offending machine. It was built in 1862 and is shown emerging from the Spencer Street locomotive sheds before going on a trial run.

This view, taken from the foot of Queen Street, Melbourne, in the 1890s gives a good idea of the range of urban and maritime transport that existed at the time.

BIRDS-EYE VIEW FROM FOOT OF QUEEN ST. WITH OLD FALLS BRIDG

Electric telegraph links were established between the capitals of the eastern colonies as early as 1859, but the continent's only source of communication with Europe were the mail and newspapers brought by the P&O clippers. The island of Java was already linked to Europe by cable and in 1870 the South Australian parliament entered into agreements with private contractors to construct a telegraph line from Port Augusta in the south to Port Darwin (then known as Palmerston) in the north, a distance of almost 3000 kilometres. It was to follow roughly the route explored by John McDouall Stuart almost a decade earlier. Separate arrangements were made for the laying of a submarine cable from Java to Port Darwin. Work began simultaneously from both ends; the project was under the supervision of Charles Todd, Postmaster-General of South Australia. After numerous setbacks, caused by the vagaries of the climate in a strange environment, the line was completed in late 1872.

The opening ritual of the enterprise (*top*) occurred on 15 September 1870, when Miss Harriet Douglas (the lady holding the mallet), a daughter of the Government Resident at Palmerston, ceremoniously planted the first pole.

The bottom picture shows Todd, second from left, and three other senior members of the expedition at the Roper River depot in 1872. Despite their studied nonchalance, the onset of heavy rain had created seemingly insuperable difficulties.

Melbourne led the way with the development of telephone services in Australia. The first exchange, privately owned and staffed by eight female telephonists, was opened in 1880 and within a year had attracted 127 subscribers. In this picture we see the telephonists — most of them recruited before the age of 18 — at work in the Wills Street exchange in 1887, the year the Victorian government took over its operation. Each call had to be answered and redirected by one of the telephonists, who frequently worked under considerable stress, having to cope simultaneously with a number of calls. It was not until the 1890s, when uncomfortable headphones supported by cumbersome breastplates were introduced, that the young women were permitted to sit down on the job.

A logical extension of the international links established by the completion of the Overland Telegraph was the laying down of a submarine cable between Sydney and Wellington, New Zealand. This put New Zealand, often referred to as the seventh Australasian colony, in direct telegraphic communication with the eastern Australian colonies and gave it access to Europe and Britain. The cable was brought ashore at Botany Bay in February 1876 from the cable-laying ship, *Hibernia*, the middle one of the three ships at anchor in the bay. Sailors haul the cable ashore, assisted temporarily and for the benefit of the camera by a number of top-hatted postal officials.

The Overland Telegraph, itself a result of McDouall Stuart's epic south-to-north crossing of the continent, also proved to be a stimulus to exploration of the western half of Australia. Ernest Giles made two successful crossings of the western half: the first in 1875, from a point a little north of Port Augusta to Perth; and the second, the following year, returning from Geraldton and crossing the Gibson Desert. This photograph is a portrait of the members of the 1875 expedition. The splendidly garbed Afghan, Saleh, was in charge of the nineteen camels that Giles decided, wisely, to take instead of horses. Tommy Oldham, the young Aboriginal in the front, was the guide. Giles is seated in the centre.

In 1870 the young John Forrest, one of the West's most important explorers and destined in his maturity to become a leading political figure, led the first successful west-to-east crossing of the southern part of the continent, following in reverse much the same route that was taken by E. J. Eyre almost thirty years earlier. In 1874 he made a more northerly crossing, beginning at Geraldton and ending at a point on the Overland Telegraph just south of Oodnadatta. The route was slightly to the south of the one that Giles would take two years later. This picture shows Forrest's party setting out from Geraldton.

The heroic exploits of the greatest explorers have never fired the national imagination as has the tragic and violent career of Ned Kelly. Kelly became a popular hero during the two and a half years he and his gang eluded the police. The myth survived his death and Ned Kelly became for many a powerful symbol of resistance to oppressive authority.

That the Kelly gang managed to remain at large for so long in a small area of northern Victoria can be attributed to their skill and determination as well as to the sympathy they inspired among many local settlers. One of the ruses to which the authorities resorted was to comb the countryside with police disguised as gold prospectors. One such group is posed in the top picture.

It was a betrayal of trust that led to Kelly's arrest and annihilation of his colleagues. Having herded the inhabitants of Glenrowan into the local inn, Kelly permitted Thomas Curnow, the local schoolteacher, to take his wife home. Curnow managed to stop a police train and inform the police of the gang's whereabouts. In the ensuing siege, Kelly was wounded and captured and the rest of the gang were either shot or burned to death when the inn was set alight. Its remains, with the sign strangely intact, are shown in the middle picture.

Joe Byrne's burnt and bullet-ridden body (*bottom*) was extracted from the building and propped up outside the Benalla gaol for the benefit of newspaper photographers and curious onlookers.

John William Lindt, whose camera recorded the gruesome scene outside the Benalla gaol on page 37, was equally at home in producing romantic studies such as this one, entitled simply *Shearing*. Its evocative background of mountains and valleys and the static pose of the shearer and the sheep give no hint of the backbreaking work that shearing was, of the struggle it often entailed between man and beast or, indeed, of the hectic conditions that typified the shearing shed. The hand shears, which were universally used until mechanical shearing began in the 1880s, and the shearer's dress are the only genuinely authentic elements in a predominantly picturesque portrait.

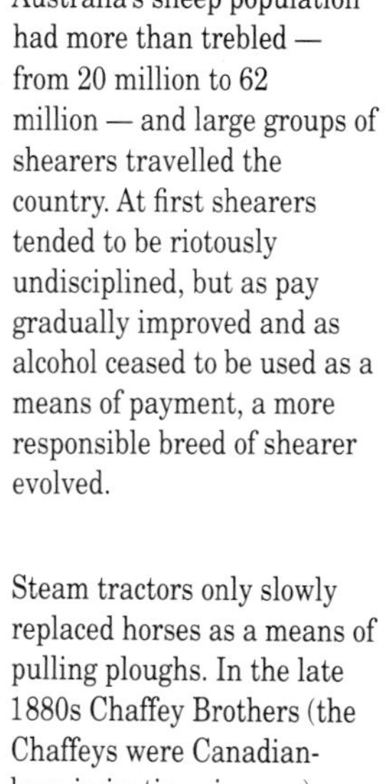

A group of shearers pose at Canowie station, New South Wales, in about 1870. Between 1860 and 1880 Australia's sheep population had more than trebled — from 20 million to 62 million — and large groups of shearers travelled the country. At first shearers tended to be riotously undisciplined, but as pay gradually improved and as alcohol ceased to be used as a means of payment, a more responsible breed of shearer evolved.

Steam tractors only slowly replaced horses as a means of pulling ploughs. In the late 1880s Chaffey Brothers (the Chaffeys were Canadian-born irrigation pioneers) introduced the first steam tractor into the irrigation area they were developing at Mildura in Victoria. Known as 'The General' this tractor is pulling two linked disc ploughs, which are breaking up virgin soil and turning a former sheep station into one of the country's most fertile and productive areas.

One of the world's first mechanical reapers was built by John Ridley in South Australia in 1843. The heads of the wheat were caught by a comb and were cut off and thrown backwards into a hopper by blades that were turned by belts attached to the wheels. Modified and refined versions of these Ridley strippers, still drawn by horses, are shown here being used in the Hammond region in South Australia in 1884.

Despite the myth that Australia is, and has been since white settlement, an egalitarian society, there has always been an enormous gulf between the rich and privileged and the poor and deprived. The pictures on these pages provide a graphic illustration of the discrepancy.

The top photograph on this page shows the family and retinue of Sir Henry Loch (the man with the beard), Governor of Victoria, at a Melbourne Cup party in 1888. Everything about the group's demeanour — and not least the seemingly conscious arrogance of the young man on the left — bespeaks the habit of ease and affluence, an impression that is reinforced by the elegance of their dress and of the setting in which they are posed.

The bottom photograph shows the drawing room of Government House, Sydney, taken in 1874. Although on a larger and generally grander scale than most, the room is in many respects typical of the drawing rooms of more affluent Victorian homes. The effect of cluttered ostentation, the profusion of ornaments and bric-a-brac, the patterned carpet and wallpaper, the moulded cornices and elaborate chandelier are typical of Victorian notions about what constituted tasteful elegance.

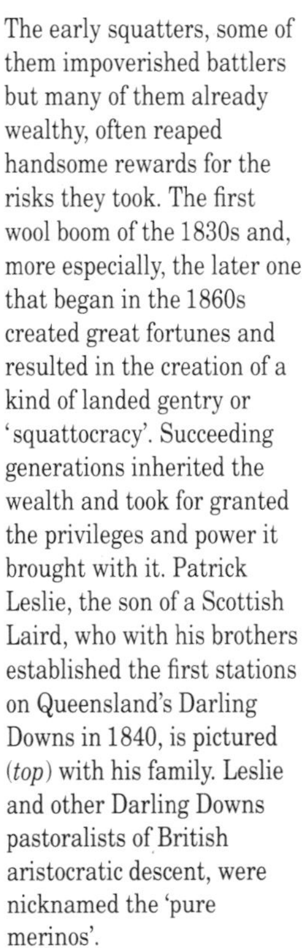

The early squatters, some of them impoverished battlers but many of them already wealthy, often reaped handsome rewards for the risks they took. The first wool boom of the 1830s and, more especially, the later one that began in the 1860s created great fortunes and resulted in the creation of a kind of landed gentry or 'squattocracy'. Succeeding generations inherited the wealth and took for granted the privileges and power it brought with it. Patrick Leslie, the son of a Scottish Laird, who with his brothers established the first stations on Queensland's Darling Downs in 1840, is pictured *(top)* with his family. Leslie and other Darling Downs pastoralists of British aristocratic descent, were nicknamed the 'pure merinos'.

Selectors, who arrived in country areas between twenty and thirty years after the squatters, were generally poorer to begin with and were often ex-goldseekers or intinerant workers who saw the availability of small holdings as a chance to put down roots and build for the future. However, the smallness of their holdings, the need to make regular repayments, their lack of farming expertise, and often the open hostility of squatters, whose land had been resumed and subdivided, created great difficulties and many of them were condemned to eke out the rest of their lives in poverty and squalor. The dwelling *(bottom)*, near Maffra in Victoria, was not untypical of the conditions that many selectors experienced.

Although a rudimentary system of public education had been set up in 1807 during Bligh's governorship, the expansion of the colony made this difficult to maintain. For most of the nineteenth century the formal education of the young was either non-existent or was provided by the church-based denominational schools that grew up after 1830 and that catered for the children of affluent parents, or by the often hopelessly inadequate national schools that were established after 1848. By 1870 all colonies had set up government-funded systems of education that were designed to make primary education available to all. One of the first of the new schools to be constructed was Sydney's Castlereagh Street Public School (*top*). Despite its fortress-like appearance, its neo-Gothic lines lent it a dignity that rivalled the grandeur of some of the affluent 'private' schools and set a standard for public school architecture in other cities and towns.

Small country towns often had to make do with a single-room school building of sometimes primitive construction, and a lack of educational resources. The district school at Lobethal in South Australia (*bottom*), built of sturdy materials and staffed by three teachers, was better than many schools in comparable communities.

The grandest Australian educational building of the Victorian era was the great Gothic University of Sydney, which was opened in 1852. Its architect was Edmund Blacket, who arrived in 1842 with almost no architectural experience. The university buildings were probably his greatest single achievement and the superb Great Hall was undoubtedly his masterpiece. The top picture, reproduced from a badly cracked glass negative, shows Blacket and his daughter standing in front of the still unfinished Great Hall in the late 1850s.

In the tradition of the Gothic cathedrals of Europe, the elaborately ornate original buildings of the University of Sydney are decorated with stone sculptures. The bottom picture shows stonemasons in the quadrangle working on gargoyles that would later be attached to the facade. The stereoscopic photograph was taken by John Smith, who was the university's first professor of chemistry and experimental physics.

On 15 February 1885, a mere four days after news of General Gordon's death during the Mahdi uprising at Khartoum had reached Sydney, the British had accepted the very precipitate offer of military assistance made by the Acting Premier of New South Wales, William Bede Dalley. Similar offers from Victoria, Queensland and South Australia were not accepted. For the first time, but not for the last, Australian soldiers were to serve in foreign parts on behalf of the British Empire, in conflicts that had no direct bearing on the defence of their native soil.

There was a rush to enlist and most of those who offered themselves for service were rejected. Those accepted included former members of the British Army who had seen recent service in Egypt, as well as raw recruits.

The hastily assembled contingent embarked on 3 March. They marched from Victoria Barracks to Circular Quay and were enthusiastically farewelled by about 20 000 cheering and singing well-wishers. The bottom picture shows the contingent moving along George Street, preceded by Dalley and other dignitaries in open carriages.

As things turned out the colonial contingent saw very little action. Three men sustained slight wounds in a minor skirmish and six others died, ingloriously, of fever. On 23 June, less than three months after leaving, the contingent disembarked in Sydney.

The idea of a federation of the six Australian colonies formed a background to all the public events of the later nineteenth century. As early as 1850 the colonial secretary, Earl Grey, had presented a draft of an 'Australian Colonies Government Act' to the British parliament, and later in the 1850s the newly arrived Irishman and Victorian parliamentarian, Charles Gavan Duffy (*bottom left*) set up a select committee to consider the subject of federation. Much of the early discussion centred around possible threats to the security of the colonies from the German and French activities in the region. Mutual suspicion between the colonial governments and an unwillingness to surrender powers thwarted these early attempts.

By the late 1880s the New South Wales Premier, Sir Henry Parkes, had become the chief protagonist of federation. At his instigation a conference was held in Melbourne in February 1890. This conference took the vital decision to set up a national convention. At this convention, in March 1891, the political momentum that would lead to the birth of a nation was created. The top photograph shows the delegates to the 1890 conference with the ageing Parkes placed dominantly in the centre.

The final stages of the path towards federation involved a series of referendums, held between 1898 and 1900, to obtain the necessary public approval. Of all the colonies Victoria showed itself to be most strongly pro-federation. The picture at bottom right shows enthusiastic Melbourne crowds at a federation rally in 1899.

2

The Federation Years

1900 – 1914

At the beginning of the period covered in this chapter Australia was at war, on Britain's behalf, in South Africa; at its close, the country was on the verge of a much greater and infinitely more destructive conflict, again in far-off places and again in the service of the Empire.

Rudyard Kipling, the arch-imperialist, novelist and poet, drew a fanciful connection between the war and Australia's achievement of nationhood. He described the new country as a 'Young Queen' on a 'red-splashed charger' riding out of battle to be crowned. Federation came irrespective of the war, and in the excited jubilation that was expressed, spontaneously and officially, right around the country there was no suggestion that nationhood had been heroically achieved or attained by the spilling of blood. The Boer War had almost universal support but Australians were far from preoccupied with it.

During this inter-war period the nation's political institutions, based on British models, were established, and groups espousing differing interests and ideologies evolved into the parties and coalitions that have dominated Australian political life. By 1910 Australia had had five Prime Ministers and seven changes of government, as the non-Labor groups — the Protectionists and the Free Traders — changed allegiances, gradually sorted out their differences and eventually fused to become a united non-Labor force.

By 1913 Canberra had been chosen as the site of the national capital and had been duly and ceremoniously named. The groups of politicians who trooped around the country, at great public expense, to inspect likely sites, fuelled the general Australian cynicism about politics and those who practise it that has persisted throughout this century.

Although the horse remained the predominant means of transportation, the motor car came of age during this period, which saw the first motorised crossing of the continent from south to north and the inauguration of long-distance car rallies. By 1910 enough private citizens were using and abusing the roads to necessitate, in New South Wales and Victoria, legislation to control their behaviour.

Previous pages: With its open verandah between two enclosed rooms, the homestead at Walla Walla station in New South Wales, pictured in 1901, is typical of many prosperous outback stations at about the turn of the century.

Left: This frolicsome trio, photographed in the early 1900s, seems to be consciously parodying the conventions of an age when going to the beach could be quite a formal outing.

Federation officially took place on 1 January 1901, the first day of the new century. It was a day of national and, by all accounts, spontaneous rejoicing, especially in Sydney where the official celebrations took place. In a specially constructed and ornate white rotunda in Centennial Park, the first Governor-General, the Earl of Hopetoun, standing in full regalia in the centre of the photograph (*top*), read the Queen's proclamation, took his oath of office and swore in the first ministry under the leadership of Edmund Barton. More than 100 000 people had stood for several hours in the hot and humid conditions to witness the historic ceremony and thousands more had lined the route of the vice-regal procession. A salute was fired and a vast chorus of 10 000 schoolchildren sang a federation anthem.

Later in the day there were various official entertainments, including banquets, fireworks displays, highland bands and, at the Sydney Cricket Ground, the schoolgirls' exhibition of maypole dancing shown in the bottom photograph. Official largesse was extended, albeit briefly, to the poor, who were provided with free theatrical performances and coupons that could be exchanged for food rations.

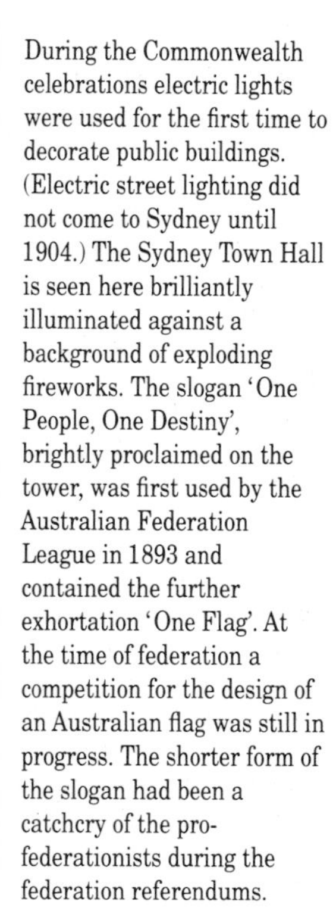
During the Commonwealth celebrations electric lights were used for the first time to decorate public buildings. (Electric street lighting did not come to Sydney until 1904.) The Sydney Town Hall is seen here brilliantly illuminated against a background of exploding fireworks. The slogan 'One People, One Destiny', brightly proclaimed on the tower, was first used by the Australian Federation League in 1893 and contained the further exhortation 'One Flag'. At the time of federation a competition for the design of an Australian flag was still in progress. The shorter form of the slogan had been a catchcry of the pro-federationists during the federation referendums.

In May 1901 the Duke and Duchess of Cornwall and York, waggishly nicknamed 'corned beef and pork', arrived in Australia to open the first Australian parliament in Melbourne. They also visited several other state capitals. These shopfronts, decorated in honour of the royal visitors with shields, flags and draperies, are on the north side of Rundle Street, Adelaide. T. Judd's bootmaker's shop has a floral welcome sign as the centrepiece of a rather gaudy and largely horticultural display. The more modestly arrayed shop of Ted Sack, the tailor, has a poster showing the duke and duchess, placed with no doubt unconscious impertinence, beside a sign advertising 'Serge suits to order 25/-'.

The ducal procession moves down William Street, Sydney, watched by a sparse crowd of onlookers. Many of them have obviously dressed up specially for the occasion; others — for example, the female domestics on the left — have simply come out to view the passing spectacle. An air of casualness is reinforced by the seeming indifference of many of the passers-by, the lack of banners and decorations and by the cyclist who nonchalantly accompanies the procession.

Despite the vigorous and almost unanimous espousal by Australia's founding politicians of a policy of racial unity — a policy that was defended with arguments that varied in tone from virulent prejudice to specious reasoning — the members of Melbourne's Chinese business community were widely respected as shrewd and successful business people.

Melburnians turned out in force to join the 'Chinese Citizens' of Little Bourke Street, who draped their shopfronts in silk and turned on a lavish parade, complete with bands of musicians, to welcome the royal visitors.

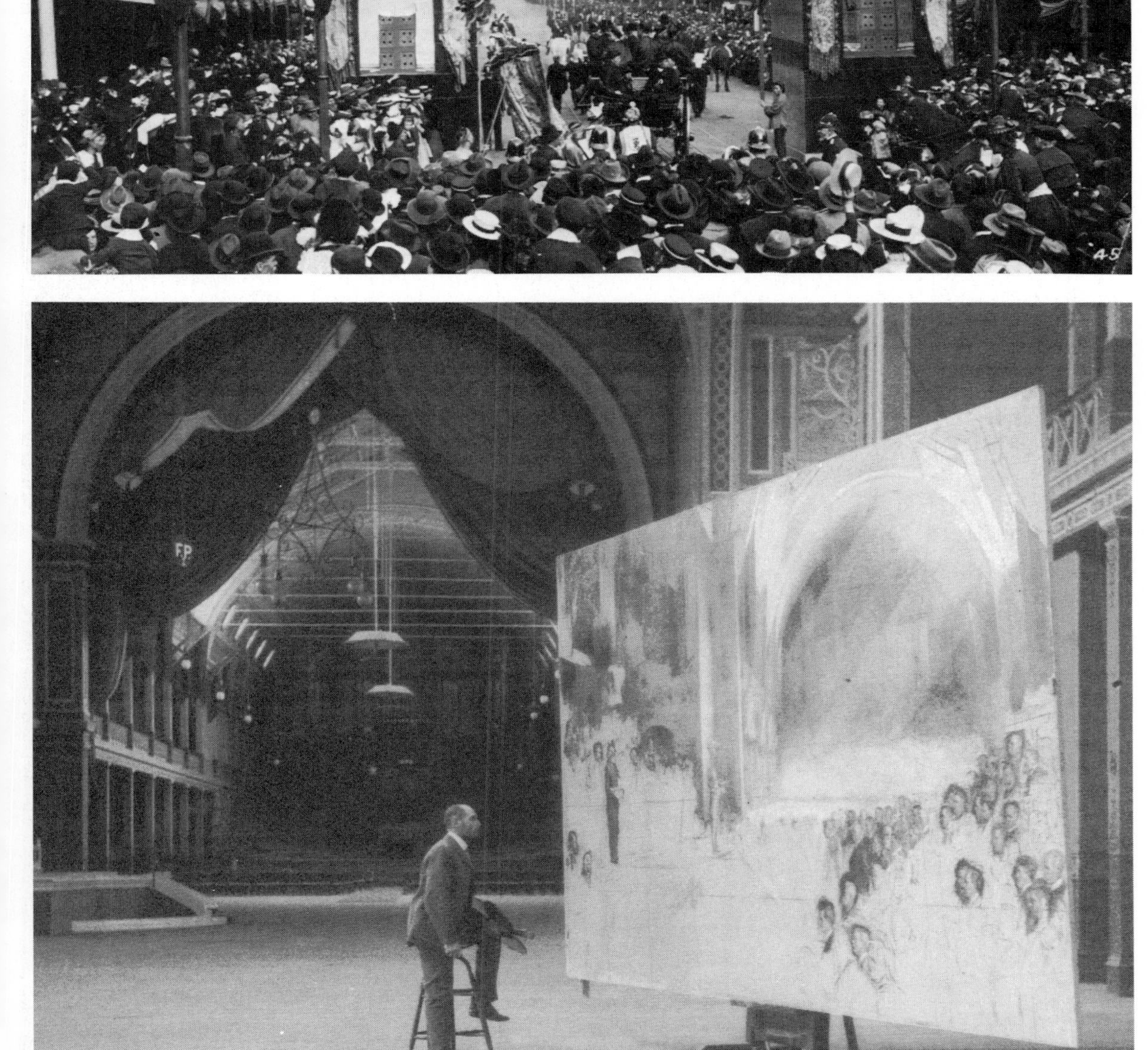

Tom Roberts poses in front of his unfinished painting of the opening of the first Australian parliament in the Melbourne Exhibition Building on 9 May 1901. Roberts, who was a noted painter of outdoor bush scenes, received a commission of 1000 guineas for the vast and uncharacteristic exercise in 'official' art, which was eventually completed in London in 1903.

Crowds turn out in Queen's Square, Sydney, in honour of Queen Victoria who died on the Isle of Wight on 22 January 1901. The Queen's statue is draped in black and surrounded by floral tributes. The buildings whose towers and domes can be seen dominating the Sydney skyline make the city one of the world's greatest repositories of Victorian architecture.

The 'White Australia' policy could, in exceptional circumstances, be overlooked, as in the case of prosperous urban Chinese and when Asians performed essential jobs that required specialised skills. Afghans, for example, remained in Australia for many years to handle the camels that were still a means of transportation in desert regions. Chinese divers, too, continued to be employed in the pearling industry at Broome in Western Australia, not so much because of their particular aptitude but because such dangerous work was left to those whose lives were considered more expendable than those of whites.

Aborigines, like other coloured races, would find scant cause for rejoicing in the constitution that came into force with the creation of the new Commonwealth. They received only two mentions and both of these were dismissive. They were specifically excluded from Commonwealth legislation and were thus made the responsibility of individual state governments, and they were not to be taken into account in assessing population numbers. By and large whites considered Aborigines to be either irrelevant or fit only for menial and servile employment. Many Aborigines in rural areas lived, like this old couple pictured with a group of South Australian station hands, in primitive conditions on the fringes of outback stations.

Fancifully entitled *Playmates*, the top photograph, taken at Derby in north-west Western Australia, shows little sign of playful interaction between the well-tailored and immaculately groomed white children and the naked Aboriginal girl. Her presence was probably tolerated only for the purposes of obtaining a picturesque photo, whose charm is, however, diminished by the sullen stares of its subjects.

The bottom photograph, taken in the Kimberley district, shows the indignities to which Aborigines in many parts of Australia were subjected in the early years of the twentieth century. At the turn of the century white settlement in the Kimberleys was still sparse and Aborigines often responded to encroachment upon their territory by spearing or stealing cattle. Suspects were rounded up and forced to work in chain gangs. The two Aborigines in European dress were referred to as 'tame boys'; they acted as interpreters between the Aborigines and their captors.

While Australia was celebrating its assumption of nationhood Australian soldiers were fighting and dying in South Africa, helping Britain to put down Boer uprisings in the Transvaal and the Orange Free State. When hostilities broke out in 1899 the colonial governments were quick to offer assistance, which was accepted with some condescension. As well as regular troops, a number of 'bushmen's contingents', consisting mainly of horsemen with little or no military experience but with an eagerness for action and adventure, were formed. The top picture on this page shows a number of these raw recruits, some of them still extremely young, at their training camp at Kensington in Sydney. In the bottom picture a bushman, mounted and in uniform, poses stiffly for the camera with his bayonet at the ready.

As they returned from the war, contingents of soldiers marched through their cities, where large crowds often gave them a hero's reception. This was followed by a ceremonial parade at which they were officially discharged from service. Returned troops are pictured here gathering at Kensington racecourse in Sydney in readiness for the parade.

The citizens of Adelaide throng the streets to welcome returning soldiers. All possible vantage points — even extremely precarious ones — have been taken. Union Jacks and early versions of the still evolving Australian flag are both in evidence.

Note that the soldiers are wearing pith helmets instead of the traditional Australian slouch hats. In many engagements during the war Australian soldiers donned pith helmets in which they were more readily distinguishable from the Boers and, therefore, less likely to be fired on in error by British soldiers.

HEADQUARTER
HEA

A group of regulars, the 1st Australian Light Horse Regiment, pose outside their Sydney headquarters after their return from service in South Africa in 1901. In spite of Britain's initial preference for infantry rather than cavalry from the colonies, Australian horsemen, both regulars and volunteers, with their experience of outback conditions, were much more of a match for the Boer than were their British counterparts and made a significant contribution to the British victory.

Despite an official reluctance by the Army Department to send nurses to the Boer War, nurses from all six colonies sailed to South Africa. Groups of nurses were attached to particular units and took their orders from that unit's commanding officer. Many Australian nurses served at the notorious hospital at Bloemfontein, where disease was rampant as a result of a water supply that had been polluted by dead horses and human excrement. The serenity and cleanliness that characterise this portrait of six South Australian nurses who went to the war contrasts with the squalor to which they would be exposed and the gruelling service that would earn three of them awards for devotion to duty.

If, as the jingoistic rhetoric of the day had it, the Boer War provided the 'blooding' that the young nation needed to prove its maturity and the opportunity for its men to show their mettle, the Australian soldiers did not fail. The 'colonials' earned the unstinting praise of Lord Roberts, Kitchener's predecessor as Commander-in-Chief, who compared them more than favourably with their imperial counterparts. Many were decorated for acts of valour and six Victoria Crosses were awarded.

In this picture Colonel Tom Price chats to Prime Minister Barton at Melbourne's Exhibition Oval before the presentation of medals to members of the Victorian Imperial Bushmen. The Countess of Hopetoun, wife of the Governor-General, is seated next to Barton.

The Disaster to Victorians at Wilmansrust, in the Transvaal.

VICTORIA MOURNS HER GALLANT SONS.

THE KILLED :—

urgeon-Lieutenant H. A. Palmer; 2, Lance-Corporal G. R. Button; 3, Private R. M. Thornton; 4, Private Archibald E. Mack (died of wounds, 16th June); 5, Private J. Collins; 6, Corporal H. Newlands;
te S. J. Barnard; 9, Private L. J. W. Goudie; 10, Farrier-Sergeant J. F. Houlihan; 11, Private R. Topham; 12, Private William A. Smith; 13, Private E. H. Blandford; 14, Private L. Bond;
ate G. W. Stratton. [Eighteen Victorians are reported to have been killed, but there has been some doubt as to the identity of two of the slain.]

In all, 16 175 men, and a slightly greater number of horses, left Australia to serve in the Boer War. Five hundred and eighteen men were killed and over 750 were wounded. Eighteen of those deaths occurred on 12 June 1901 during an incident at Wilmansrust, in the eastern Transvaal, an incident in which the Australians — members of the 5th Victorian Mounted Rifles — did not cover themselves with glory and which led their British commanding officer to describe them as 'a fat-arsed, pot-bellied, lazy lot of wasters'. While searching for a Boer commando unit the Australians had pitched camp, had posted their lookouts in full daylight and had stacked their rifles at some distance from their tents. Soon after nightfall the Boers they were seeking staged a surprise attack. As well as the dead, more than 60 Victorians were wounded.

This collage of portraits was published soon after as a solemn memorial of the tragic event. It contains portraits of sixteen of the dead. At that stage the other two had not been identified.

Although the motor car was to become a revolutionising force in Australia and in comparable societies, and by the 1920s would be a widespread means of independent mobility, in the first few years of the century it was still predominantly a novelty. Many of the early cars were one-off models built for the owner's exclusive use; often they were experimental, not to say eccentric, in design and construction and were put together by enthusiastic amateurs, with bicycle parts and other materials that were to hand.

The two less-than-sturdy-looking South Australian vehicles pictured on this page more or less fit this description. The car in the top picture was built in 1901 by an Adelaide bicycle manufacturer and seems to have been the only one of its kind. The car built by Fred Modistach of Tanunda in 1903 (*bottom*) clearly betrays its bicycle origins.

This car, completed in 1903, was for a number of years a feature of the Lithgow district in New South Wales. It was in effect a motorised horse buggy with a lever rather than a steering wheel and solid wheels that must have made for rough travelling over the unmade country roads.

By 1905 enough motor cars had been imported into Australia to satisfy the demand by the relatively few people who could afford them. Depending on their size and make cars cost between £300 and £800 and, according to one contemporary newspaper, would soon be accessible to almost 'every squatter and well-to-do farmer'. In March 1905 the Automobile Club of Australia was formed to lobby for better conditions and fewer restrictions on motorists, whose noisy and polluting vehicles could play havoc among older and more sedate forms of traffic. Although for the time being debarred from ownership, the public at large were fascinated by the new machines and when, in February and November 1905, the Dunlop Rubber Company sponsored two motoring contests between Sydney and Melbourne general interest was keen.

These two contests were the precursors of later reliability trials, with the drivers required to cover sections of the route within specified time limits. The condition of the main roads ensured that both cars and drivers were tested to the utmost. The second contest, which began in Melbourne, could only be decided after the leading six cars, out of a total of 28, were sent on a return journey. It became a major newspaper event.

The picture shows a French de Dion car throwing up clouds of dust after negotiating a corner during the first contest, from Sydney to Melbourne.

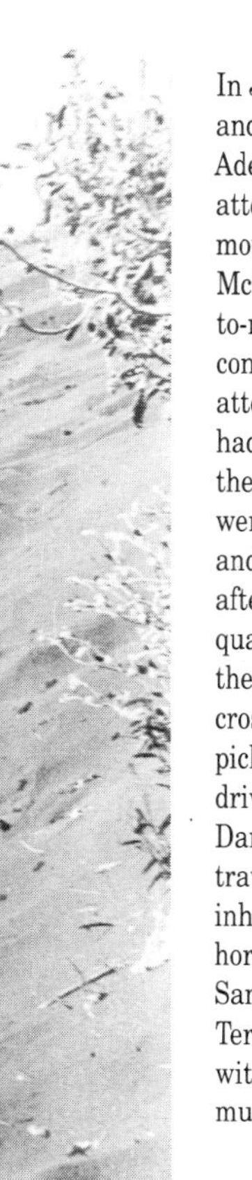
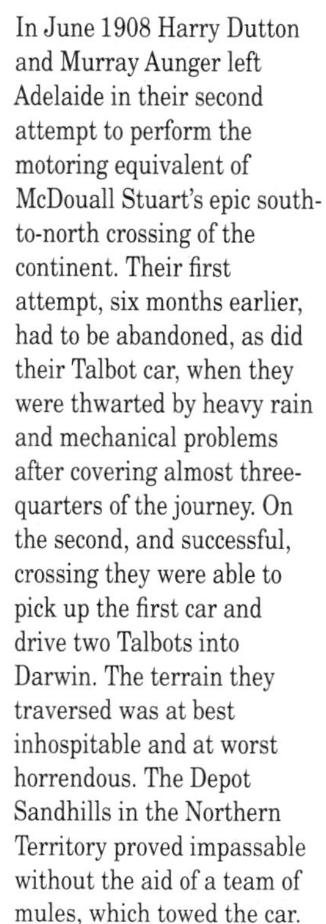

In June 1908 Harry Dutton and Murray Aunger left Adelaide in their second attempt to perform the motoring equivalent of McDouall Stuart's epic south-to-north crossing of the continent. Their first attempt, six months earlier, had to be abandoned, as did their Talbot car, when they were thwarted by heavy rain and mechanical problems after covering almost three-quarters of the journey. On the second, and successful, crossing they were able to pick up the first car and drive two Talbots into Darwin. The terrain they traversed was at best inhospitable and at worst horrendous. The Depot Sandhills in the Northern Territory proved impassable without the aid of a team of mules, which towed the car.

An obviously well-heeled family with their top-of-the-range de Dion car in about 1910. By this time the number of cars on the roads was sufficient to cause concern about the hazards they represented, and collisions and other accidents, sometimes fatal, were no longer uncommon. Matters were not helped by the vagueness of speed limits, which in Sydney varied from one municipality to the next, and by the crassly irresponsible driving habits of some car owners. In about 1909 both the New South Wales and Victorian parliaments sought to regulate driving behaviour by introducing motor traffic bills.

Horse-drawn coaches such as this one photographed in about 1908, which carried passengers between Newcastle and the coastal resort of Port Stephens in New South Wales, were still used for reasonably long journeys that were not serviced by the railways. Much faster motor cars, overtaking vehicles like these, would often startle the horses and add to the already considerable discomforts of the trip by showering the exposed passengers and driver with clouds of dust.

Horse, pedal, electric and leg power predominate in this scene, looking east from the intersection of King William, Hindley and Rundle streets in Adelaide in 1909. One could easily imagine that the motor car had not been invented, and the roadways seem to be used almost as freely by the pedestrian as the vehicular traffic. The electric trams had only recently been introduced and in 1909 were running on only one route. They would eventually replace the distinctive double-decker horse-drawn trams, such as the one in the foreground.

By 1909, when this picture was taken, the river traffic on the Murray-Darling-Murrumbidgee system had declined dramatically from its peak in the 1870s and 1880s. The expanding railway system had taken over much of the paddle-steamers' role as passenger and cargo carriers. The river traffic, although reduced in volume, survived throughout the twentieth century and has had a recent revival as a tourist attraction. The *Ruby* pictured here was the fourth steamer to bear that name. It was built at Morgan in 1907 and carried passengers and cargo between Morgan and Swan Hill. By the 1970s the *Ruby* had been converted into a museum boat, stationed at Wentworth.

The advent of steamships brought a gradual phasing out of the great sailing clippers. Until well into the new century, however, sail was still used to convey both passengers and cargo across the seas.

This photo shows a ship ready to leave Bundaberg in Queensland in the early 1900s. It is taking Pacific Islanders who are being forcibly repatriated in accordance with the government's 'White Australia' policy. Since the 1870s people from the Pacific Islands had been brought into Queensland as a source of cheap labour for the sugar plantations. Although many of them were cruelly exploited the decision to send them all home by the end of 1906 brought protests, not only from disgruntled plantation owners, but also from many Islanders who wished to remain.

Getting the woolclip away was vital both to the station owners whose livelihood depended on it and to the new nation for which wool was still by far the greatest export earner. While most of the wool reached the major cities by rail, large and heavily laden wool wagons were still a familiar sight in the outback, as they transported the bales from the stations to the railheads. Teams of horses were most commonly used to pull the load. In the top picture two teams stand ready to take loads from Goombargoona station, New South Wales, in 1901. Bullocks, and sometimes mules, as in the centre photograph, were also put to work in the service of the wool trade.

Barges, drawn by paddle steamers, continued to be an important form of transportation from stations along the Murray-Darling-Murrumbidgee systems. The bottom picture shows a barge, stacked to capacity, on the Murray in 1910.

The 1880s and 1890s were boom times for the sheep industry and by 1891 the number of sheep in Australia had risen to 106 million. By this time, however, the limits of sheep-grazing land had been reached and the former rate of expansion could not be maintained. A persistent drought in eastern Australia that began in 1895 and reached its peak in 1902 reduced the number of sheep by almost half. By 1902 there were only 54 million. Cattle numbers, which had grown to 12 million by 1894, were also halved.

The pictures on this and the following two pages show a number of scenes on New South Wales sheep stations in 1901. Even though the largest properties were in Queensland, New South Wales' extensive and fertile western plains were the nation's most prolific source of wool. By the mid-1890s the state had about 40 large sheep stations, some of which contained more than 100 000 sheep.

This picture shows sheep being 'dipped' at Walla Walla station. The sheep are being individually manhandled from the pen into the trough. The man looking towards the camera is ready to prod any sheep that may be reluctant to move.

A skilled shearer would begin by tossing a sheep on its back and removing the wool from its belly. Then, in one continuous movement, the wool from the two flanks and the back would be removed in a single fleece. The need for constant stooping took its toll, especially on the back muscles, as did also the steamy heat that was generated inside the galvanised-iron shearing sheds.

The shearer in this shed is still using hand clippers, even though belt-driven mechanical shears, invented in the 1880s, were now widely used. A top shearer, using hand clippers, would shear more than 100 sheep in a nine-hour day, and tallies of more than 200 were not unknown. Mechanisation made possible individual scores of more than 300 in nine hours.

A group of shearers pose during a 'smoke-oh' pause outside the shed at Round Hill station. The device attached to the pole was known as a 'whip' and was used for lifting the wool bales onto wagons.

Even into the twentieth century shearers were predominantly a solitary breed. Few travelled with such 'encumbrances' as a wife, and women were rarely encountered in the often primitive shearers' huts.

After being shorn and sorted, the wool was packed into large hessian sacks bearing the name of the station and then pressed into bales ready to be transported. This picture shows the wool press at Walla Walla station. The press was operated by bringing considerable force to bear on the large wheel that the man on the platform is holding. The station manager, standing third from left, and whom we saw on the opening pages of this chapter looking every bit the overbearing paterfamilias, here assumes another appropriately authoritarian stance.

Whereas sheep were restricted to relatively grassy areas, cattle, with their greater capacity to travel to water and to graze off less well-covered land, were being successfully, if not all that efficiently, bred in some fairly arid parts of the inland in the early 1900s. Between 1900 and 1910 the number of cattle in the Northern Territory rose from a quarter to just over half a million. The fact that herds of cattle could be walked, rather than transported, overland to market also contributed to their being raised in more remote regions.

The top photograph, taken in 1908, shows the very arid-looking Horseshoe Bend station on the Finke River, south of Alice Springs in the Northern Territory. Life, it would seem from the look of the buildings and the landscape, would have been rugged in such an environment. At least the motor car, on which a man can be seen working in the middle foreground, would have alleviated some of the problems by making the more distant parts of the property more easily accessible.

A more gracious style of station life could be achieved in more fertile areas, where often extensive gardens were cultivated and carefully maintained, especially in the vicinity of the homestead. Large and prosperous properties sometimes employed a sizeable gardening staff. The ten gardeners (*bottom*), looking a trifle country-bumpkinish with their implements thrust to the fore, were all employed on one South Australian property in 1902.

Gracious living was certainly enjoyed at the Camden Park Estate in New South Wales. This property was owned by the Macarthur-Onslow family, and comprised the land granted to Captain John Macarthur in 1805 where he experimented with the cultivation of wool.

Members of the Macarthur-Onslow family and members of their staff are seen enjoying one of the rather formal but lavish picnics that were a popular pastime of the well-to-do. Mrs Elizabeth Macarthur-Onslow, the granddaughter of John Macarthur, is side-on to the camera in the lighter costume and dark hat; her daughter, Sibella, nurses the family's pet dog.

At the other end of the social scale, this German immigrant family, comprising a farmer, his careworn wife, eleven children and two pet dogs, stand on their recently cleared land in front of a simple slab cottage at Hahndorf, south-east of Adelaide. The land was made available under the 'closer settlement' legislation that was enacted in South Australia in 1897 and more or less contemporaneously in the other colonies. The rifle that the farmer is holding was probably the means of procuring much of their food. The home-made toy rifle that the child between the two adults is cradling in his arms was no doubt one of the very few playthings the family could afford.

In the early years of public and compulsory schooling, education tended to be a very rigid and formalised process, limited to the acquisition of little more than the 'three Rs'. Things began to change during the 1900s. Between 1905 and 1913 in New South Wales, for example, a new, broader curriculum that included subjects such as nature study and science and stressed the importance of learning through direct experience, was introduced into primary schools. After 1911, too, a new system of secondary schooling, designed to cater for different levels of ability and interests, was introduced. The majority of children, however, stayed at primary school until they left at the age of fourteen.

The three pictures on this page are propaganda photographs designed to promote the new and more relaxed approach. The photographs at the top and bottom right were both taken in 1913 and show the same class of children, at Cleveland Street Public School, learning respectively by the old, supposedly outmoded, methods and by the new progressive ones. The bottom left picture, taken in 1910 at Kurri Kurri Public School, demonstrates a 'hands-on' approach to learning geography. In case the message is not clear enough, it is spelt out on the board in the foreground.

This photograph charmingly captures the excitement of the little South Australian girl as she prepares to ride her new tricycle. Dress in the early 1900s was very much an indicator of social class and prosperity, and even children at play were often arrayed in what today seem excessively elaborate clothes. The lace trimmings, the fine cut of the dress and the sturdy boots all stamp this child as the daughter of well-off parents. They contrast sharply with the plainness of the clothes worn by the Hahndorf children on page 75.

At the turn of the century Australian capital cities, and especially Sydney and Melbourne, were marred by slum areas that were as insalubrious as they were depressing. The state of these slums was forced onto the attention of the authorities when an outbreak of bubonic plague occurred in Sydney's Rocks and Darling Harbour areas in 1900. The City Council reacted in a decisive and, some thought, excessively heavy-handed manner, quarantining the areas, disinfecting houses with little regard to the scant possessions of the occupiers, and ruthlessly pulling down decrepit outhouses and lavatories.

The top picture, taken in 1901, still presents a depressing scene. Next to the run-down Whalers' Arms Hotel is a vacant block where a condemned building has been demolished. A few locals pose idly for the camera. At bottom left is the back of some terraces in Cumberland Street which were condemned and demolished.

The outbreak was thought to have been started by rats that came ashore from ships berthed at the Darling Harbour wharves. A campaign was launched to eradicate as many as possible of the rats in the area and out-of-work men were employed as rat-catchers. At bottom right we see a group of these men with their day's catch.

Despite all these moves the outbreak was not contained. It spread to all other states except Tasmania and persisted until 1907, by which time more than 1100 had been infected, and more than 500 had died of the disease.

In December 1908 another serious outbreak, this time of industrial trouble, occurred in the western New South Wales mining town of Broken Hill. The immediate cause of the trouble was the decision of the Broken Hill Proprietary Company, which operated one of several mines in the town, to reduce its miners' wages by removing a 'bonus' that had been paid since 1906. Tensions in the town were already running high and for some months there had been rumblings about working conditions. Ill-feeling was further provoked by the state government's action in sending 50 Sydney policemen to Broken Hill to stave off trouble. The ensuing strike, known locally as 'the Lockout', lasted until May 1909 and was marked by bitterness, outbreaks of violence and permanent dislocation of many miners' lives. The miners' victory in the courts — the wage cut was restored after much legal wrangling — was largely negated by BHP's refusal to reopen its mine. At the end of the dispute less than half of the 3000 strikers had jobs to go back to.

A great deal of the miners' hostility was directed against strikebreakers or 'scabs'. They took a vicarious revenge by hanging the offenders in effigy or by constructing mock graves, like the one in this photograph made out of an iron bed frame, with appropriately threatening inscriptions.

It was stipulated in the Constitution that the national capital was to be situated within New South Wales but outside a radius of 100 miles (160 kilometres) from Sydney. Although Barton had promised an early decision on the matter the parliament was unable to agree; places as far afield as Albury and Armidale were suggested. Between 1903 and 1908, when Canberra was finally decided upon, groups of politicians travelled to the various proposed sites to survey their potential.

One such group is seen here at Albury clowning for the camera. The large man awkwardly astride the fence is Sir William Lyne, a federal minister and the former Premier of New South Wales. Immediately to the right of him is William Morris Hughes.

On 13 March 1913 a 'Commencement Ceremony' was held on the slopes of Capital Hill. Three foundation stones for the national capital were laid — by Lord Denman, the Governor-General; by the Prime Minister, Andrew Fisher; and by King O'Malley, the Canadian-born Minister for Home Affairs. Lady Denman made the first public announcement of the name of the new capital. The area had previously been known as Canberra, but rumours abounded that it might be called something outrageous like 'Sydmeladperbrisho', in deference to all the states; or, if O'Malley had got his way, 'Shakespeare'. The photograph shows the official guests dispersing after the ceremony.

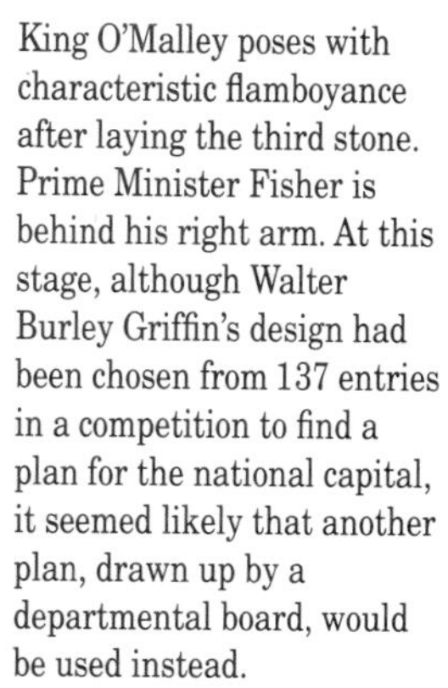
King O'Malley poses with characteristic flamboyance after laying the third stone. Prime Minister Fisher is behind his right arm. At this stage, although Walter Burley Griffin's design had been chosen from 137 entries in a competition to find a plan for the national capital, it seemed likely that another plan, drawn up by a departmental board, would be used instead.

Racist sentiments received an airing in two speeches at this ceremony. O'Malley spoke of English-speaking people ruling Australia 'in the interests of civilisation' and Hughes, then Attorney-General, smugly noted the absence of members of 'that race we have banished from the face of the earth'.

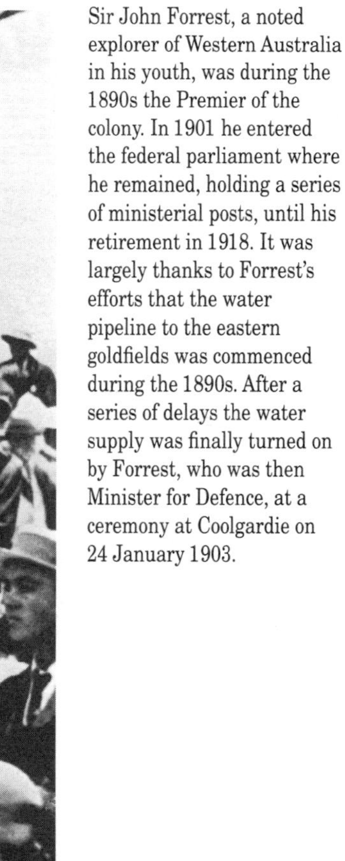
Sir John Forrest, a noted explorer of Western Australia in his youth, was during the 1890s the Premier of the colony. In 1901 he entered the federal parliament where he remained, holding a series of ministerial posts, until his retirement in 1918. It was largely thanks to Forrest's efforts that the water pipeline to the eastern goldfields was commenced during the 1890s. After a series of delays the water supply was finally turned on by Forrest, who was then Minister for Defence, at a ceremony at Coolgardie on 24 January 1903.

Walking races were a popular form of sporting activity in the early 1900s and were often a prominent feature of large group outings and picnics. They were an exclusively male preserve and involved a degree of undress not then considered becoming for women. Some events aroused considerable public interest. People have turned out in some force to follow this race at Glen Osmond in South Australia in July 1903. One of the contestants is in the foreground, surrounded by supporters.

Crowds jostle for the best vantage point on the banks of the Parramatta River near Sydney to watch two Australians compete against each other for the sculling championship of the world in July 1904. So great was interest in the event that about 90 000 people turned out to see it. While most clambered over the banks or climbed trees to get a view, a few more privileged enthusiasts paid as much as a pound to watch the race from the deck of a ferry. In the early 1900s sculling was a popular recreational and competitive sport and regattas drew large crowds of spectators.

About 1910, when this photograph of Sandringham Beach in Victoria was taken, the cult of the sun had not yet come to Australian beaches. Prevailing standards of dress ensured that even when swimming most of the body remained decently covered.

A visit to the beach was as often as not for the purpose of taking the sea air and only the more hardy actually got wet. They would arrive fully dressed and change in the seclusion of the changing sheds on the right. Mixed bathing, unheard of a decade earlier, was still considered by many to be immoral and an affront to female modesty. In 1911 the Catholic Archbishop of Sydney created quite a furore when he referred publicly to it as 'offensive generally to propriety' and in particular because of its 'attraction for idle onlookers'.

Tennis was a game in which the sexes could safely mingle; both men and women played the game covered completely from neck to ankle, and female athleticism was effectively curbed by flowing skirts and petticoats. Cricket, though less common, was also sometimes played by women. This photograph, taken by William Henry Corkhill, shows the members of the Tilba Tilba ladies cricket team, dressed with varying appropriateness, in about 1905.

3

World War I

1914 – 1918

Almost 60 000 Australians, most of them young men with a taste for adventure, died in World War I. Another quarter of a million were injured, some of them permanently maimed. Romantic myth and stark reality were never thrown into sharper contrast than in Australia's responses to the Great War.

The men who enlisted in a surge of patriotic feeling and imperial loyalty, and with starry-eyed notions of military glory, had their ideals shattered in the ignoble slaughter at Gallipoli and in the putrid, muddy trenches of Belgium and northern France. Australians at home seized on the Gallipoli campaign, stripped it of its terror and ugliness, and in their imaginations turned a futile, ill-conceived and tragically wasteful defeat into a glorious vindication of the national spirit. Here, indeed, was nationhood finally earned. Gallipoli entered the national psyche as the most powerful of all Australian myths.

The palpable suffering and grief that the war produced, however, gradually had its effects on the public reaction to it. Twice the Australian people rejected the proposal that their young men should be conscripted for overseas service, despite well-orchestrated and highly emotional appeals to their sense of patriotism and the persuasive powers of William Morris Hughes, a popular and determined Prime Minister.

Conscription, the most controversial and rancorously fought issue in the history of the young nation, split the Labor Party, caused its leader to defect — his Prime Ministership still intact — and kept it out of power for another twelve years.

It has been claimed that the spectre of Asian immigration was behind Hughes' fanaticism about conscription. He feared that if Britain had to rely on Japanese rather than Australian support she would in turn bring pressure to bear on Australia to allow Japanese to migrate. To this Hughes was adamantly opposed.

While the war preoccupied Australians it did not divert them from the pursuit of their own domestic interests. Industrial action in support of higher wages was taken by New South Wales coalminers in 1916, and in 1917 an extended strike by railway and tramway workers about administrative procedures soon involved a wide cross-section of the union movement, brought many community services to a halt and disrupted shipping — in Hughes' words, 'the very life's blood of the Empire' — for several weeks.. Occurring at a time of national crisis it was seen to be the most damaging strike in Australia's history.

Previous pages: Australian troops trudge wearily towards the front through the slushy mud of a devastated landscape at 'Idiot Corner', Passchendaele, Belgium, in October 1917.

Left: For many of the volunteers who enlisted in the Australian Infantry Forces the war seemed to offer the chance of a great adventure. The carnival atmosphere that characterised some early embarkations is typified in the brisk gait and high spirits of these Sydney soldiers being farewelled by their girlfriends.

War was declared on 4 August 1914 and the next day Australia promised to place 20 000 troops at Britain's disposal. Recruiting began a week later and the first Australians to serve in the major theatres of war sailed, from Albany in Western Australia, on 1 November. Early recruiting was brisk. Young men, blissfully unaware of the horrors ahead and nurturing romantic ideals of heroism and adventure, rushed to enrol. By the end of the year almost two and a half times the promised number of men had joined up. Many more, failing to meet the stringent fitness standards, had been disappointed. These volunteers are receiving their recruitment papers at a recruiting office in Melbourne.

This rather motley-looking group of West Australian volunteers is on parade at their training camp at Blackboy Hill, near Perth. They would soon be in uniform and off to the war. Of almost 25 500 West Australians who embarked for the war 70 per cent were killed or wounded. A higher percentage of West Australians than of men from any other state were killed in action, or by other misadventure, during World War I.

Members of the 12th Battalion march through Hobart on 20 October 1914 on their way to embark for the war. These men were among the first Australians to leave for the war and would sail from Albany in Western Australia with other Australian troops and a contingent from New Zealand. Crowds jam the streets and occupy every possible vantage point to give the soldiers a rousing farewell. In all about 12 200 Tasmanians went to the war; just over 20 per cent did not return and another 40 per cent were wounded in action.

Towards the end of August 1914 a small force of about 2000 volunteers left Sydney by sea for New Britain in German New Guinea. In this photograph a part of the Australian fleet gathers off the Louisiade Archipelago on 9 September 1914 to provide cover for the forthcoming operation in Rabaul. In the foreground is the submarine *AE I* and in the distance are the battle cruiser *Australia* and the destroyer *Yarra*.

The scene below decks in the mess of HMAS *Australia*.

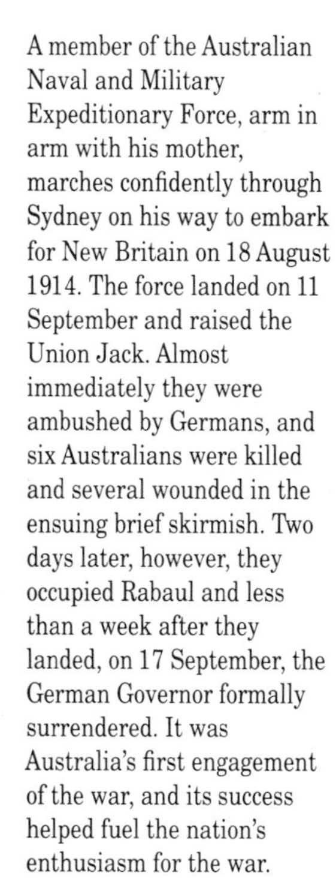

A member of the Australian Naval and Military Expeditionary Force, arm in arm with his mother, marches confidently through Sydney on his way to embark for New Britain on 18 August 1914. The force landed on 11 September and raised the Union Jack. Almost immediately they were ambushed by Germans, and six Australians were killed and several wounded in the ensuing brief skirmish. Two days later, however, they occupied Rabaul and less than a week after they landed, on 17 September, the German Governor formally surrendered. It was Australia's first engagement of the war, and its success helped fuel the nation's enthusiasm for the war.

Another early incident that stirred Australians' patriotism and created a good feeling about the war was the disabling, on 9 October 1914, of the German cruiser *Emden* by HMAS *Sydney*, one of the ships escorting the convoy of Australian troops that had left Albany eight days earlier. The *Sydney* intercepted the *Emden* preparing to destroy a vital cable station on Cocos Island in the Indian Ocean. The staff of the cable station, aware of the impending attack, had sent a wireless message, which was relayed to the *Sydney*. It left the convoy and engaged the German ship, which was crippled and forced ashore on Keeling Island. Three Australian seamen were killed and 15 wounded in this first Australian naval engagement of the war. The *Emden* had acquired a fearsome reputation because of the 23 ships it had previously destroyed.

The top photograph shows the *Sydney* under full steam during the raid on Rabaul on 11 September 1914. In the bottom photograph sailors in one of the *Sydney*'s boats approach the *Emden* on the day after the engagement to take off the survivors, who can be seen gathered on the stern.

A procession farewells volunteers from the New South Wales country town of Tumut during the first flush of enthusiasm for the war in 1914.

The huge throng that watches this military parade, passing in front of St Andrew's Cathedral in George Street Sydney on Australia Day 1915, indicates the fervour with which the public supported Australia's participation in the war.

25 April 1915 was to be one of the most significant days in Australian modern history, not because of a solid achievement but because it was the beginning of a horrific bloodbath that left almost 9000 Australians, and 3000 New Zealanders, dead, and that quickly became a symbol of young and valiant nationhood. On that day, beginning at 4.29 a.m., 16 000 members of the Australian and New Zealand Army Corps — to be known forever more as Anzacs — made a series of landings at Gaba Tepe on the Gallipoli Peninsula in Turkey. The Australian landings had been met by fierce Turkish resistance from entrenched positions on the high and rocky coastline. The aim of the exercise — one that was not achieved — was to support a simultaneous British and French attack further to the south in an attempt to drive the Turks from the peninsula.

The top photograph shows the scene at what later became known as 'Anzac Cove' during the first days after the landing. Tents have been erected on the beach and a jetty has been constructed to facilitate the landing of supplies. Several men are bathing naked in the sea, guns are being moved along the beach and a group of soldiers in the left foreground survey the rocky and steep terrain. Men making their way up from the beach (*bottom left*) were forced to take shelter behind scrub and in natural depressions in the hillside. Water, shipped in tanks from Egypt, had to be dragged laboriously up the hill (*bottom right*), always under the threat of enemy fire.

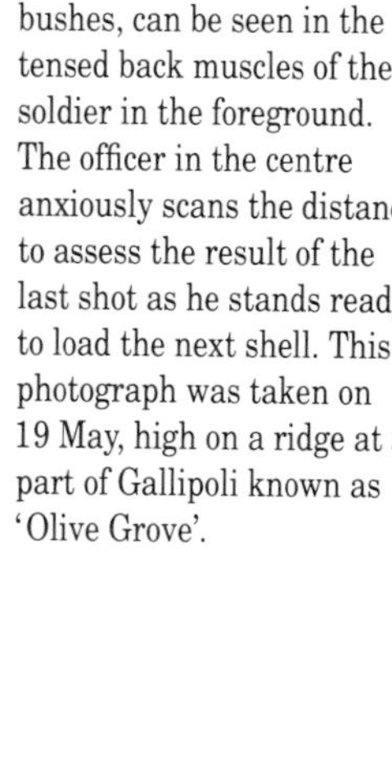

The strain of firing this 18-pounder, concealed under bushes, can be seen in the tensed back muscles of the soldier in the foreground. The officer in the centre anxiously scans the distance to assess the result of the last shot as he stands ready to load the next shell. This photograph was taken on 19 May, high on a ridge at a part of Gallipoli known as 'Olive Grove'.

Entrenched behind walls of sandbags, these Australian soldiers, manning a sniper post, use rifles fitted with periscopes to get the enemy in their sights. These invaluable devices were the invention of an Australian soldier, Lance-Corporal W. C. Beech.

For a week after the landing the Anzacs and Turks struggled for possession of the ridges overlooking Anzac Cove. Much of the area changed hands several times before the Anzacs were able to establish entrenched positions. This grim scene shows the bodies of Turkish soldiers, killed during an offensive at a place called 'the Nek'. Both sides are taking advantage of a brief truce to collect and bury their dead.

This picture of Chunuk Bair Ridge to the north-west of Anzac Cove, where the Anzacs staged an unsuccessful attack on the night of 6 August 1915, while a British force made a landing several kilometres further north, gives a clear idea of the rugged, rocky and scrubby nature of the area in which the long Gallipoli campaign took place.

Left: Private J. S. Kirkpatrick of the 3rd Field Ambulance was known as 'the man with the donkey'. With his donkey he shepherded wounded men from the hills and ridges to the beach from where they could be taken out by boat. Always in danger from enemy fire, Private Kirkpatrick was killed by shellfire on 19 May.
Right: As the weeks wore on the weather became steadily hotter; flies invaded the trenches and infested the dead and smelling bodies that sometimes lay for days inside and on the edge of trenches.

Perhaps the most famous single battle during the eight-month Gallipoli campaign was the storming and capture, at a tremendous cost in lives, of Turkish trenches at a place evocatively named 'Lonesome Pine'. The attack began at 5.30 p.m. on 6 August, when successive waves of Anzacs went 'over the top' and stormed what they had thought to be open Turkish trenches. To their amazement and initial confusion they found that the trenches were roofed and protected with solid logs and that they had to lower themselves in through narrow openings. By 6 p.m. the battle was over and the Anzacs had secured the position, which they managed to hold despite six days of Turkish counter-attacks in which handgrenades were extensively used. This photograph, showing men occupying one of the fortified trenches several days after it had been captured, was taken by C. E. W. Bean, Australia's official war correspondent and later the compiler of an Australian history of the war. Bean was wounded during this engagement in which Australians earned seven Victoria Crosses.

NUGGET
AUSTRALIAN MONT DE PIETE LOAN & DEPOSIT Co
KINO'S
MERCHANT
TAILORS
W.A.A.C.
FOR EMPIRE

In white blouses and black skirts, members of the Women's Auxiliary Army Corps brave the rain to march through Melbourne in support of the war. Their banner proclaims the patriotic slogan 'All for Empire'.

As in all wars rumours about the nefarious deeds of the enemy abounded and a good deal of hysteria was generated about the dangers, real or imagined, of 'aliens' within Australia. People of German birth or extraction were often subjected to physical and moral intimidation. One incident that helped to inflame anti-alien opinion occurred at Broken Hill, where, on New Year's Day 1915, two Turks fired on a train full of picnickers, killing four and wounding seven. The two offenders were soon disposed of by a vigilante group. That evening an incensed mob converged on the local German club, burnt it to the ground and, in a rush of irrational fury, set off to exterminate the Afghans in the nearby 'camel camp'. Only the intervention of local citizen forces prevented a massacre.

Almost 7000 of the 33 000 people classified as 'enemy aliens' spent most of the war in special internment camps that were set up in each state. The three top pictures show scenes at Torrens Island camp in South Australia. The top right photograph is of the camp choir. This camp was closed in 1915 and its inmates transferred to Sydney. The two bottom pictures were taken at a camp at Berrima in New South Wales. The one on the left shows the bar at the camp, and in the photograph on the right three young German girls pose with their teacher. The overwhelming majority of internees were men; only 67 women and 84 children were interned.

People who did not have relatives or close acquaintances serving in the forces remained reasonably detached from the war. It was a long way away and, apart from an occasional propagandist scare about dangers to Australia, most Australians at home felt no real threat. Schools, like other social institutions, continued to operate. This school at Chakola in New South Wales, photographed in 1918 with its full complement of pupils of varying ages and its single teacher, was typical of many small schools in country areas.

In 1916 Sydney's zoo was transferred from its previous site at Moore Park to its harbourside setting at Taronga Park. One of its best known attractions was Jessie the elephant, seen here in a photograph by Harold Cazneaux with her load of excited young passengers. Jessie continued to give rides for another 18 years and eventually died just two months before the outbreak of the next great global conflict.

While most Anzac troops were moved to the Western Front, in France and Belgium, during 1916, some remained to fight the Turks in the deserts of Sinai and Palestine. In the spring of 1916 Australian and New Zealand mounted troops were involved in operations east of the Suez Canal. In August they distinguished themselves in the battle of Romani by withstanding a fierce attack by 18 000 Turks. Their progress eastwards across the desert depended largely on the progress of a water pipeline that was being constructed from Kantara on the Suez Canal. Here Australian troops water their horses in the Sinai desert.

In December 1916 the Imperial Camel Corps was formed under the command of Brigadier C. L. Smith. More than half its members were Australians, and many of them had previously served in camel companies in the eastern Sinai. On 23 December the Camel Corps and other Anzac mounted troops were victorious in a battle at Magdhaba near the Palestine border and on 9 January they won another encounter at Rafa in eastern Palestine.

In the last year of the war Anzac troops in the Middle East fought in the Jordan Valley in hot and dusty conditions, sometimes plagued by malaria, as they slowly gained ground against the Turks. These members of the Light Horse take cover, their bayoneted rifles at the ready, as they await a Turkish attack. Hand-to-hand encounters were frequent and troops were issued with swords as well as rifles and bayonets. At this stage of the war most British troops had been moved to the Western Front and the Anzacs were joined by troops from India, the British West Indies, Algeria and South Africa as well as by two Jewish battalions.

These Turkish prisoners, being guarded by members of the 3rd Light Horse, were captured in a surprise evening attack on the town of Es Salt, east of the Jordan, on 30 April 1918. However, a Turkish counter-attack forced the Anzacs to withdraw several days later. There were to be five more months of fighting before Turkey finally surrendered in October 1918.

When the convoy of ships taking the first Australian troops to serve overseas left Albany in Western Australia on 1 November 1914, it carried with it a group of 24 women. They were members of the Australian Army Nursing Reserve and were the first of about 3000 Australian nurses who served abroad during World War I. They were sent to all the major theatres of war and staffed a number of stationary and base hospitals. Many of them served at the hastily established hospitals on islands such as Lemnos and Mudros where casualties from Gallipoli were brought and treated in hot and fetid conditions.

In the top photograph is a group of Australian nurses at the Salonika front. In winter, these 'Salonikans', as they called themselves, had to treat, as well as injuries, some heartrending cases of frostbite. The bottom photograph shows a group of nurses at the No. 1 Australian Stationary Hospital at Ismailia, Egypt, early in 1916. The uniforms worn here were adopted during World War I; they replaced the much more cumbersome ones, with huge capes and ribboned bonnets, that had been standard up till then. Thirteen Australian nurses, ten of them from Victoria, were killed during service in World War I.

Women contributed to the war effort in a great variety of ways. As individuals and as members of voluntary organisations they raised money, collected clothes, knitted garments and organised food parcels to be sent to the troops. All the departments of education encouraged pupils, especially girls, to knit socks, gloves, scarves — anything that might improve the lot of the far-off soldiers. The almost one and a half million pairs of socks that were knitted helped reduce the incidence of 'trench foot' that resulted from standing in the muddy trenches at the Western Front. In Melbourne the Red Cross was allowed to take over the ballroom of Government House for war relief work (*top*). The St John Ambulance Brigade was one of many organisations whose members (*bottom left*) made clothes for soldiers.

The photograph of the incongruously dressed little boy (*bottom right*) was part of a campaign to encourage support for the war effort.

The initial flush of enthusiasm for the war had subsided by the end of 1915. For one thing, the novelty of being at war had worn off and the hoped-for quick, decisive victory had not eventuated. Perhaps more importantly, an understanding of the sordid reality, as opposed to the heroic myth, of modern warfare had begun to dawn on the mass of Australians. Gallipoli had been glorious — but had been a failure — and the glory had been hard won. Reports of the extent and the nature of casualties had been bad enough, but the real and palpable grief of families that had lost sons, or whose sons had been irretrievably maimed, was becoming more and more evident. The return of wounded and incapacitated servicemen, like this blinded young soldier, also added to the general disillusionment.

Scenes like this became more common as the war wore on. These people have gathered outside the *Argus* building in Melbourne on a Sunday morning to await the war news and casualty lists.

In 1916 the number of volunteers who enlisted dropped by almost a quarter and, with the numbers being killed and wounded, it was becoming increasingly difficult to maintain the level of Australian forces. The Labor government, under William Morris Hughes, wanted to resort to conscription to fill the shortfall. A referendum to win popular approval for the proposal was held in October 1916 and was narrowly defeated. Hughes' own Labor Party split over the issue of conscription, and Hughes and 22 Labor members of parliament left the party and formed a coalition government with the Liberal Party. In December 1917, with enlistment declining even more drastically, another referendum was held. The result was the same, but this time more decisive. Here Hughes, with typically theatrical gestures, addresses a conscription rally in Martin Place, Sydney.

In 1917 recruitment had dropped to just over 45 000, less than half the unsatisfactory 1916 figure. Conscription had been rejected and the government was reduced to employing a bewildering range of gimmicks in order to build up its forces. Individual citizens and 'patriotic' groups did their bit by bringing subtle and blatant pressure to bear on those who were thought to be shirking their duty. White feathers were sent through the post and fit-looking young men were ostracised in the street. At the official level, posters, some of them crudely xenophobic, were printed and prominently displayed, and exhortatory speeches were made. Every attempt was made to keep the matter firmly in the public eye and to exert the maximum moral pressure — like the New South Wales recruiting train *(top)* bedecked with flags, slogans and royal portraits, and the parade of banner-bearing recruits *(bottom)*.

In this publicity shot, a young and 'fit' man, in smart civilian dress, and with his hat tilted carelessly back to suggest an air of casual irresponsibility, is confronted with his duty by soldiers in uniform.

While the government was trying to maintain public support for the war effort, a radical organisation with anarchist tendencies, the Industrial Workers of the World, was adopting a loud, if rather ineffectual, anti-war stance. The contention of the extreme left-wing group, which at its height could muster no more than 2000 Australian members, was that the war was being promoted by capitalists for their own ends. It also strongly advocated violence as a means of changing the social order. The government was so provoked by the IWW's propaganda that in 1917 it declared the organisation an 'unlawful association' and had its members gaoled. This photograph shows members of the IWW, generally referred to as 'wobblies', at a rally in the Sydney Domain in 1915.

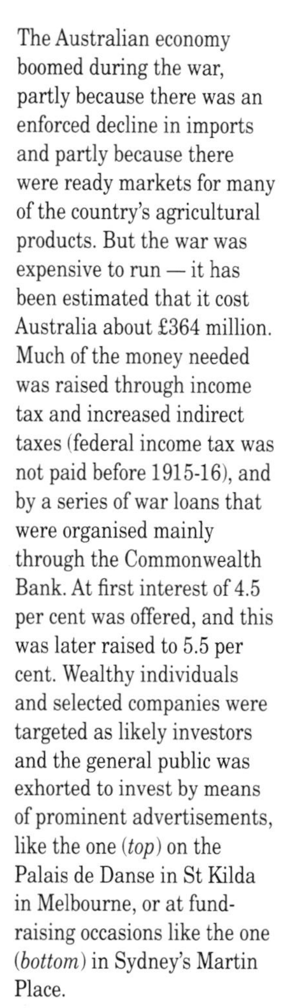

The Australian economy boomed during the war, partly because there was an enforced decline in imports and partly because there were ready markets for many of the country's agricultural products. But the war was expensive to run — it has been estimated that it cost Australia about £364 million. Much of the money needed was raised through income tax and increased indirect taxes (federal income tax was not paid before 1915-16), and by a series of war loans that were organised mainly through the Commonwealth Bank. At first interest of 4.5 per cent was offered, and this was later raised to 5.5 per cent. Wealthy individuals and selected companies were targeted as likely investors and the general public was exhorted to invest by means of prominent advertisements, like the one (*top*) on the Palais de Danse in St Kilda in Melbourne, or at fund-raising occasions like the one (*bottom*) in Sydney's Martin Place.

In March 1916 the first Australian troops sailed for France to fight on the Western Front. They began arriving in April and saw their first action in July on the Somme and at Fromelles. These members of the 6th Brigade, their hats and helmets held jubilantly aloft on the points of their bayonets, seem genuinely happy to have arrived at last in Flanders. Within the space of two short weeks, between 25 July and 7 August, 1900 of them would be killed at Pozières.

Left: Sir George Reid, who had been Australia's Prime Minister for eleven months in 1904-05, and who had recently completed a six-year term as Australia's first High Commissioner in London before winning a seat in the House of Commons, stands stiffly to attention as he addresses Australian soldiers newly arrived in north-eastern France.
Right: The Australian Prime Minister, Billy Hughes, was in England for the first half of 1916 where he was fêted by royalty, the aristocracy, politicians and businessmen, and where he received extravagant praise in the press. In the midst of this heady excitement he visited the Western Front.

In this apparently idyllic scene Australian soldiers play cards in a field, while French children sit idly by. In the background there is a busy movement of war equipment and supplies along the road. The truck advertises the apéritif, Dubonnet, which seems almost consciously to point up the irony of the scene.

One of the Australian organisations, run almost entirely by women, that was dedicated to providing food and clothing to troops at the front was the Australian Comforts Fund. Here Australian soldiers on the Somme in 1916 find some relief from the physical discomfort of their surroundings and the horror of the trenches in coffee sent to them by the Australian Comforts Fund.

These wounded Australians resignedly await the arrival of ambulances after their successful capture of the Menin Road bridge, over the River Lys, during the third battle of Ypres on 20 September 1917. One soldier, blinded in the action, stares blankly ahead as he walks with the support of two comrades. Another, apparently unwounded, soothes his nerves with a hastily poured drink.

The ravages that war has brought to the vegetation of the area are poignantly highlighted by the dead horses and splintered carriage in the foreground of this photograph, which shows the 1 Anzac Corps moving along the road between Ypres and the Menin Road bridge in September 1917. This particular spot became known, not inappropriately, as 'Hellfire Corner'.

Left: On 20 September Australian troops near Ypres staged successful attacks against German positions, at the cost of over 5000 casualties. Under heavy artillery cover they stormed German trenches and dislodged the enemy from the concrete pill-boxes in which they took shelter. Here German and Australian dead lie in front of an abandoned pill-box.

Right: In the midst of the carnage there is still time for emergency dental work.

Australian troops have taken possession of this solid German-built dugout, with its timber support and vaulted brick ceiling, in Ypres during the assault on Passchendaele in late 1917. The superficial jollity conceals the weariness the men must have been feeling, and the fact that the struggle for Ypres and Passchendaele, which had dragged on for three months in a constant quagmire, had meant the loss of 38 000 Australian men.

The breaching of the Hindenburg Line, the extensive series of reinforced trenches the Germans had set up east of the Somme, in October 1918, was the final major offensive of the war and the one that marked the end of effective German resistance. Here Australian troops and British tanks attack German positions near Bellicourt on 29 September. It was one of the last actions of the war in which Australians took part.

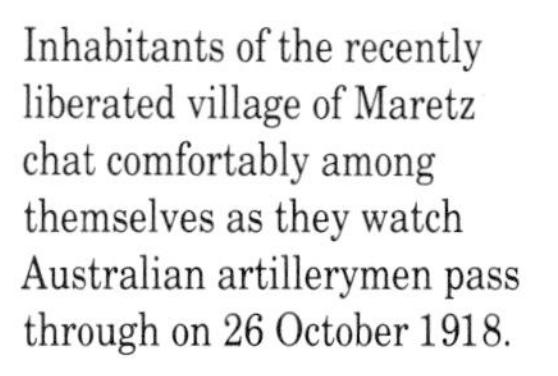

Inhabitants of the recently liberated village of Maretz chat comfortably among themselves as they watch Australian artillerymen pass through on 26 October 1918.

Between March 1916 and March 1917 four squadrons of Australian airmen were formed. The No. 1 Squadron, which included Captain Ross Smith, who would later make the first flight from England to Australia, made important contributions to the campaigns in Sinai and Palestine. The other three squadrons all trained in England and later served in operations on the Western Front.

The top photograph shows Australian airmen and some of the machines they flew during training at Minchinhampton in England in 1917.

In the centre photograph men of the No. 4 Squadron stand around a strategically placed bomb to have this picture taken in France in 1917.

In the bottom picture Australians stand proprietorially around a captured German aircraft which made a forced landing behind Australian lines east of the Somme in August 1918.

Spontaneous demonstrations of joy and relief, like this one in Martin Place in Sydney, erupted in cities and towns all around Australia on Armistice Day, 11 November 1918. In some cases the crowds' enthusiasm degenerated into mob disorder, as in Melbourne where tramcars were derailed and shopfronts smashed.

Suspense is clearly written on the faces of these people as they tensely scan the decks of a troopship for their first glimpse of returning loved ones. The young woman in the front has temporarily forgotten the box Brownie camera she has brought in order to record a hoped-for reunion, and the old woman beside her holds a flag ready to wave at the moment of recognition. Even the very small child in the left background has caught the air of anxious expectancy.

Reunited with his rather overwrought-looking wife and three children, this soldier, with his kitbag balanced carelessly on one shoulder, returns to domestic life, sound in limb and, it seems, in mind. Others, maimed or blinded in action, had less cause to be sanguine about the future. Many of them, rendered unemployable by the war, would be reduced to begging in order to live.

This carefully composed and evocative photograph by Harold Cazneaux, taken in 1918, is entitled *Peace after war, and memories*. The lonely figure pausing behind his primitive plough in an almost bare landscape powerfully expresses the sense of loss and disorientation that many returned soldiers experienced. Presumably a soldier settler, this man, like many others who took up land after the war, would have to struggle to make a living in an unfriendly environment.

Hughes, who had been absent from Australia since April 1918, and who would not return until the following June, is triumphantly borne aloft by jubilant Australian soldiers in London on 11 November 1918. Hughes demanded, and won, separate representation for Australia at the Paris Peace Conference, which culminated in the signing of the Treaty of Versailles. In so doing he took the first step along the path that eventually led to Australian independence in foreign policy.

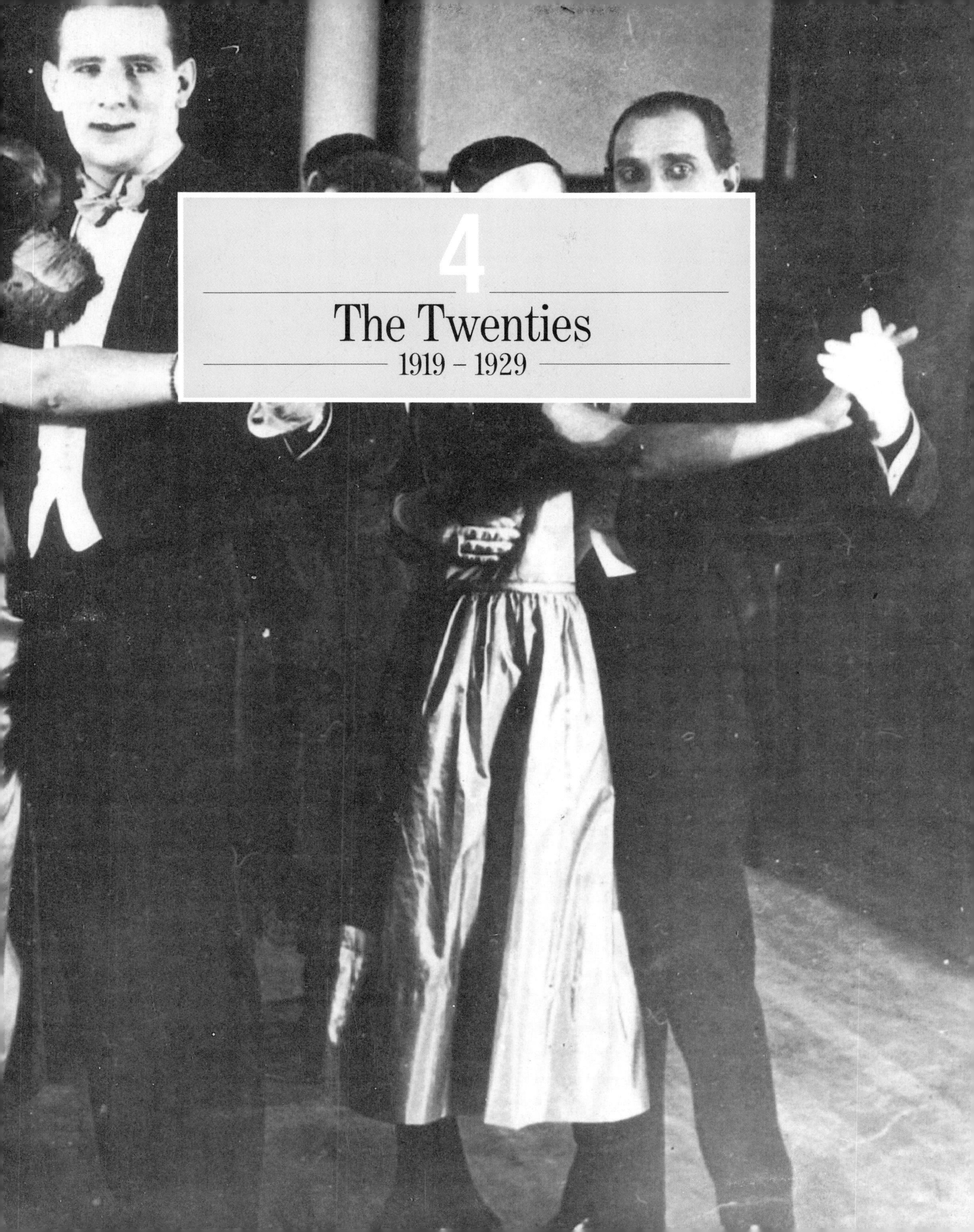

4
The Twenties
1919 – 1929

The twenties, popularly regarded as a decade of untrammelled well-being, was, for many Australians, a time of trial and difficulty. The period was framed by misfortune. From late 1918 to early 1920 the whole country, but especially New South Wales, was affected by the influenza epidemic that was sweeping the world and which, as it was probably brought in by returning soldiers, was a further tragic legacy of the war. Over 12 000 Australians died in the epidemic, a high proportion of them in their twenties and thirties. And at the end of the decade the dramatic Wall Street crash heralded the onset of the Great Depression.

Throughout the 1920s unemployment remained high — in part as a result of the large influx of surplus labour after the war — and poverty was widespread if not always conspicuous. Improvements in pay and working conditions were hard to come by in the face of the largely unsympathetic attitude of the conservative government led by Stanley Bruce and, after 1925 particularly, strikes were frequent. The rapid mechanisation of industry, too, condemned many workers to the inhuman drudgery of the production line. The formation of the Australian (originally Australasian) Council of Trade Unions in 1927 resulted in a generally more unified and more effective union movement.

Two new political parties — the Country Party and the Communist Party — were formed in 1920. The former was to play a vital role in shaping Australia's political future and the latter, while never attracting more than a tiny minority of the population, would be the centre of repeated and heated controversy during the next half-century. In the 1920s the mass electronic media were born and the increasing popularity of the cinema and the advent of radio significantly altered the entertainment habits of most Australians. Domestic comfort was enhanced by the availability of electric power, for lighting as well as to run an ever-increasing range of labour-saving devices. Gas, telephones and the extension into many suburban areas of the main sewer also helped to make life more congenial for those who could afford them.

The mass production of cars brought private motorised transport within the reach of a greater number of people. By the end of the decade there was one car for every twelve people in Australia. An expanding system of air services brought important and welcome changes to life in remote outback areas.

Previous pages: The popular image of the 1920s, epitomised in pictures such as this, was one of continuous good times.

Left: Slum dwellings like these, associated in the popular imagination more with the 1930s than the 'roaring twenties', showed the other, and perhaps more realistic, side of the coin.

In the general euphoria that greeted the end of World War I in 1918, it would have seemed unimaginable that the great conflict had still not run its destructive course. In January 1919 outbreaks occurred in both Sydney and Melbourne of a deadly strain of influenza, known as 'Spanish influenza'. It was part of a worldwide epidemic and was probably brought into Australia by servicemen returning from the war. By the time it had run its course, early in 1920, it had claimed the lives of more than 11 500 Australians, and in Sydney more than one-third of the population had been infected. Steps to stop the spread of the disease included the discouragement of public gatherings and the closing of schools and libraries. Even churches were closed for a time; when they were reopened church-goers were required to sit a metre apart. For most of 1919 people had to wear masks when they were out of their homes.

In Sydney an Influenza Administration Committee, staffed mainly by volunteers who travelled around in special 'SOS' vehicles, was set up to monitor the situation of poor and elderly people. The top picture shows a group of these workers. In most capital cities, and even at state borders, quarantine camps were established to remove those suspected of being infected from contact with the community. The bottom picture shows the quarantine camp at Jubilee Oval in Adelaide.

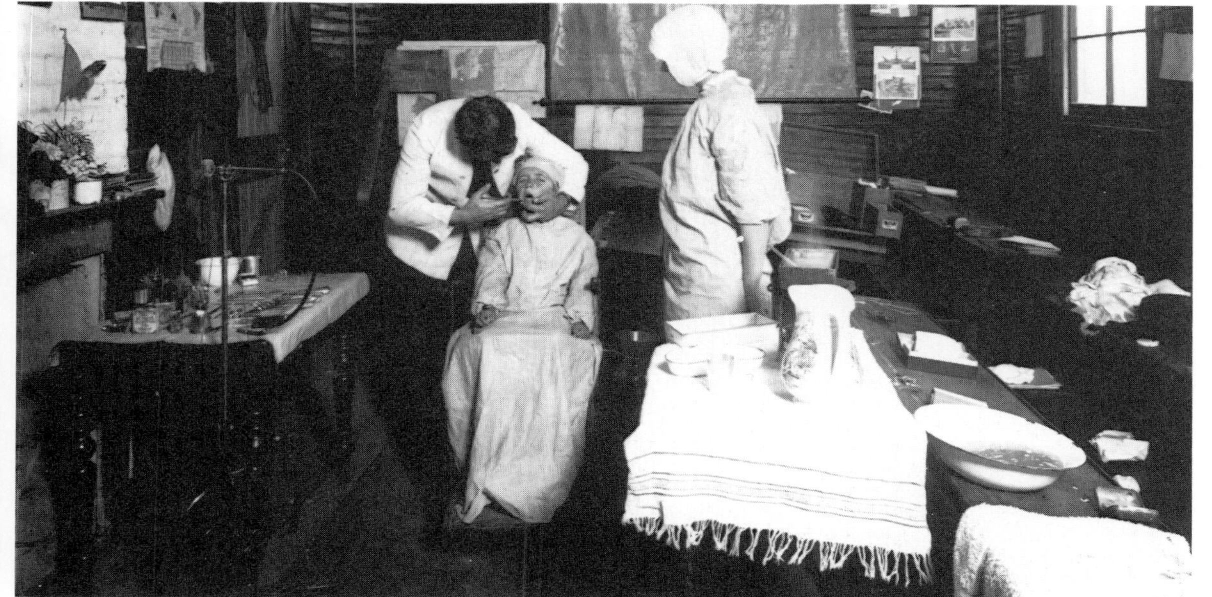

The wholesale slaughter of young life that occurred during World War I, as well as the influenza epidemic of 1919, probably helped to reinforce a growing community awareness of the importance of health and nutrition. The influenza scare provided a boon for the manufacturers and promoters of a range of dubious medicines and preventatives. Schools often led the way in encouraging more reliable methods. The top picture shows free milk being distributed to young children at the Blackfriars Infants School, in the centre of one of Sydney's poorer areas, in 1923.

By the 1920s dentistry was the exclusive preserve of qualified practitioners. Legislation had put an end to the unscrupulous methods of quack dentists who had operated freely up to the end of the war. Schools were visited by itinerant dentists who often set up temporary surgeries in classrooms. The bottom picture, taken at a school at Budgee Budgee, near Mudgee in New South Wales, gives an idea of the state of dental technology in the 1920s. The pedal-operated drill might have caused older patients than this one to experience a few nervous twinges.

After World War I returned soldiers were given the opportunity to take up blocks of repurchased or crown land and to develop these for agriculture. This soldier settlement scheme was financed jointly by the state and federal governments. The scheme was not markedly successful and many of the resettled farmers had left their land within a few years. In some cases the failure resulted from a combination of unsuitable land, high cost of equipment and lack of farming expertise. This West Australian farmer has clearly made little impression after four years of effort.

The difficulties their parents are having making ends meet are reflected in the ragged dress of most of these settlers' children, many of them without shoes and obviously wearing hand-me-downs. They are photographed with their teacher outside their rough bush school, built in a clearing in the West Australian bush. In comparison with his charges, the youthful teacher looks positively elegant in his decently plain suit and tie.

Two institutions that belonged to a former age but that survived into the age of motorised transport were the travelling school (*top*) and the horse-drawn ambulances (*bottom*). Between 1908 and 1923 three vehicles like the one in the top picture trundled around the north of New South Wales bringing the first glimmerings of enlightened literacy to the children of families in isolated places. The small wagons served as home and storeroom to the itinerant teachers whose job involved the exercise of a considerable range of pedagogic, survival and, on occasions, veterinary skills. A tent, which could be used as a classroom if necessary, was included as part of the equipment.

The advent of motor transport gave a boost to what had previously been fairly primitive and uncoordinated ambulance services. The first ambulances in Australia were organised by the St John Ambulance Association, which was formed in Melbourne in 1887. This was followed by the formation of the St John Ambulance Brigade, which, along with other voluntary groups, was operating in the 1890s, transporting sick and injured people, first in simple two-wheel buggies, and later in more commodious and better equipped vehicles like the ones in the bottom picture.

Many soldiers who took up the government's offer of land after World War I received a rude shock when they arrived at their allotments, some of which were in remote and relatively inaccessible areas. Some, expecting to find land already under cultivation, were dispirited to discover that their block was uncleared, unfenced and contained no buildings. With money borrowed from the government they purchased what farming equipment they could afford. It was seldom the latest technology, and mechanical traction for their ploughs was a luxury they could only dream of. The settler (*top*) is using an outmoded plough to cultivate his land in the Mallee District of western Victoria.

For the more affluent landholders, with larger acreages, exciting and much more efficient new forms of traction were becoming available. Graceless and noisy monsters they might have been, but huge diesel-powered tractors, like the Melbourne-built McDonald Imperial Diesel (*bottom*) pictured in about 1925, could perform the work of about a dozen horses. The sheer bulk of these tractors made them relatively unsuitable for areas with heavy soil and on small properties. By 1928 South Australia had just over two and a half thousand tractors in regular use and in 1930, two years after its formation, the Victorian Tractor Owners' Association had twelve branches throughout the state.

One of the greatest scourges to afflict Australian agriculture was the spread of prickly pear, a South American native cactus that was brought to New South Wales as a pot plant in 1839. Its true destructiveness became obvious only when it increased rapidly after the breaking of the 1902 drought. By 1925, about 25 million hectares, equivalent to the combined areas of Scotland and Wales, of choice farming and grazing land had been overrun. The introduction of the Argentinian insect, *Cactoblastis cactorum*, in the late 1920s eventually stemmed the tide and by 1930 the pest had been virtually beaten. This photograph shows an infested property in Queensland in the mid-1920s.

Drought is probably the most pervasive and persistent of the natural disasters that regularly afflict Australia. Extended periods when significant areas of the continent have been free of drought have been rare in the period since white settlement brought agriculture to this country. Between 1918 and 1920 there was a major national drought and for most of the 1920s important areas were affected. In 1927 north-western Victoria and South Australia were particularly hit. The effects of drought, exacerbated by years of poor soil management, is dramatically demonstrated in this 1920s photograph of an exposed tree root in Victoria's Mallee District.

By the 1920s the motor car had ceased to be a novelty and, although it remained the preserve of the well-to-do, it was no longer merely the plaything of the very rich. Indeed, by the end of the decade the number of registered motor vehicles had increased tenfold and mass production had greatly reduced the cost of owning a car.

This picture, taken at Sydney's Bondi Beach on a Sunday in 1929, gives some impression of the extent of private car-ownership by the end of the twenties and of the inconveniences that Sunday driving could entail.

Trucks began in the twenties to replace horse-drawn wagons for the delivery of goods and also provided an admirable form of mobile advertisement. Trucks, proudly proclaiming the products of their owners, and often bearing eye-catching samples of the signwriter's art, became a common sight in city and suburban streets. Some of them drew public attention to small enterprises such as a local bakery; others, like this early Arnott's van, displayed the famous trademarks that had become national symbols of their products.

Touring buses allowed for quick and relatively comfortable forays into the countryside by large groups of people. A day tour from Sydney to the Blue Mountains, for example, in a vehicle that could go directly to the major sights, was for many a more attractive prospect than a train trip followed by a number of subsidiary journeys. This picture shows the members of the Commonwealth parliamentary staff, some of them bizarrely disguised, on a 'Pioneer' bus outing near Melbourne in 1926, the year before the opening of the new Parliament House in Canberra.

Essential public services that relied on fast transportation received a great boost from the advent of motorisation. Although the first motorised fire-fighting machine was used in Australia as early as 1902, and services were gradually converting to petrol-driven fire engines, it was not until the twenties that these became widespread. Canberra's first fire engine shows the state-of-the-art equipment towards the end of the 1920s.

By 1927, fourteen years after its official commencement ceremony, only slow and painful progress had been made on the construction of the national capital. Its designer, Walter Burley Griffin, had long since fallen foul of the bureaucrats and had resigned the supervision of the project. The city itself consisted of little more than the buildings of the Civic Centre, a few residential and government buildings and the new 'temporary' Parliament House, built as a stopgap until something more suitable could be completed. It was opened with appropriate pomp on 9 May 1927 by the Duke of York, whose father — now King George V — had presided over the opening of the first parliament in 1901, and who would himself become King George VI.

This picturesque arch, its columns consisting of stacked wool bales, was one of several inspired by agriculture that adorned the city of Brisbane during a visit in 1920 by the Prince of Wales, who would later become King Edward VIII.

On 7 April 1927, just a month before the opening of the nation's Parliament House, the Duke and Duchess of York, looking decidedly more relaxed than do their modern counterparts in similar situations, walk through the grounds of Brisbane's Parliament House after attending a reception in the chamber of the Legislative Council.

Contrasting aspects of the opening of Parliament House. On the left, the great Australian operatic soprano, Dame Nellie Melba, now nearing the end of her career, sings 'God Save the King' while Prime Minister Stanley Bruce stands solemnly to attention. On the right a lone Aboriginal sits forlornly in a field with a few belongings and his two dogs. His race would find small comfort in the sentiments expressed during the ceremony. The Prime Minister in his speech looked forward to a future in which 'millions of the British race will people this land'.

Dame Nellie Melba — she was created a Dame Commander of the British Empire in 1918 — was the most renowned operatic soprano of her day. Her career spanned almost forty years and her operatic association with the great Italian tenor, Enrico Caruso, was legendary. Her association with the country of her birth, however, was at times ambivalent; legend has it — and the story may be apocryphal — that when the British singer Dame Clara Butt was embarking on a tour of Australia Melba advised her to 'sing 'em muck! It's all they can understand'. In spite of this she returned to Australia to give her last operatic performance, as Mimi in *La Boheme*, in 1928. Here, at the end of the performance, in Melbourne's Her Majesty's Theatre, she stands impassively among streamers and floral tributes to acknowledge the audience's emotional response.

In 1926 another peerless performer, the Russian ballerina Anna Pavlova, toured Australia. This portrait by Harold Cazneaux, a study in serene grace, was taken on stage before the curtain went up at Her Majesty's Theatre in Sydney.

Curiously, both artists had more in common than their prodigious talent: they both had desserts named after them — the pavlova was invented and named in Australia in 1935 and the peach Melba was created by a French chef in 1893 — and both died in 1931.

During the 1920s moving films, universally referred to as 'the pictures', emerged and then firmly consolidated their position as the predominant form of mass entertainment. A thriving local film industry grew up for a time, only to be eclipsed by a flood of American films that were imported, especially after the advent of 'talkie' films towards the end of the decade.

The most enduring Australian film of the era, and one that was to become accepted as a classic of the silent screen, was *The Sentimental Bloke*, based on C. J. Dennis's poem and made by Raymond Longford in 1919. The top photograph shows Arthur Tauchert, with bowler hat and cigarette, as The Bloke. Tauchert also played in another notable Australian silent film — *For the Term of His Natural Life* — based on Marcus Clarke's historical novel about convict life in Port Arthur. He is in the left foreground of the still from that film reproduced in the bottom photograph.

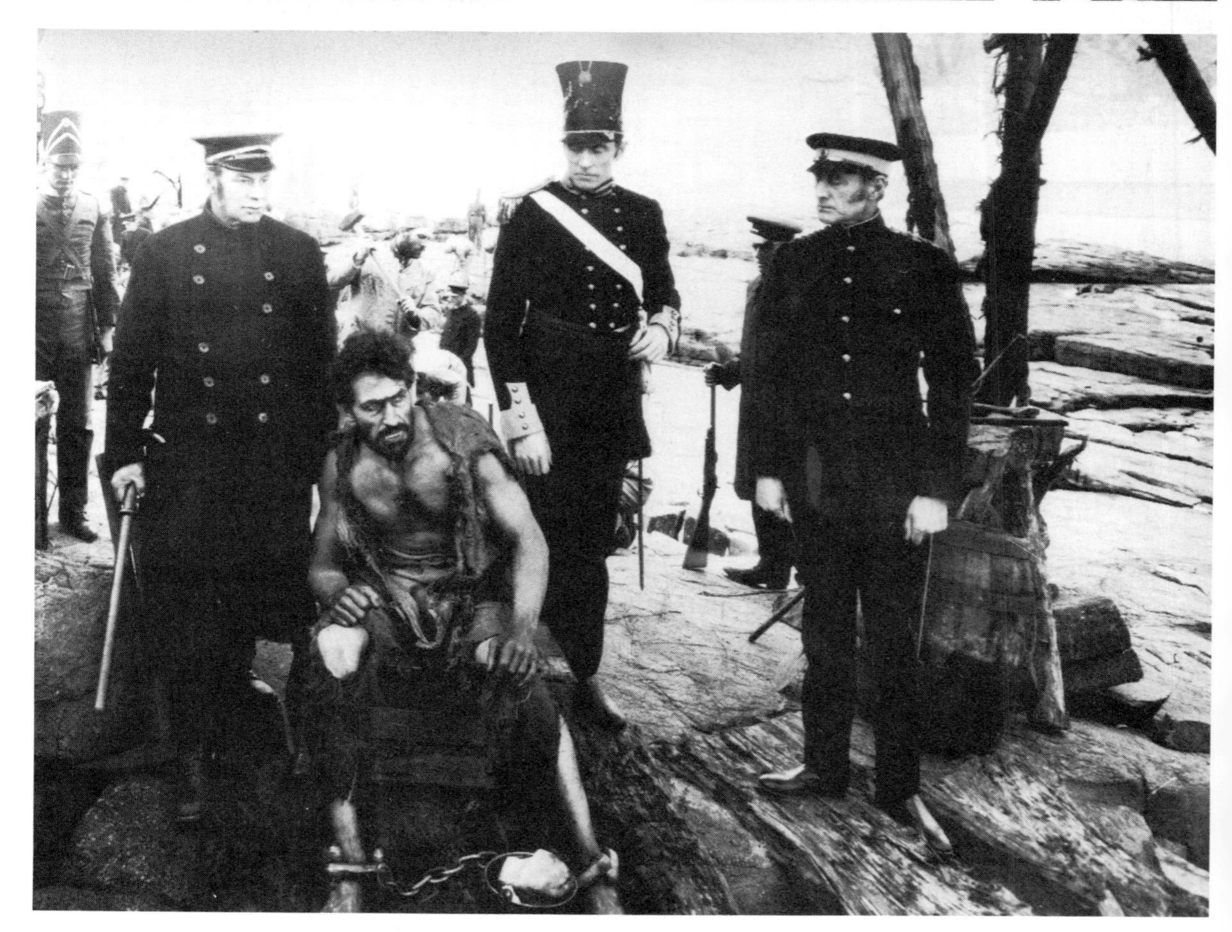

In many respects the Capitol Theatre in Melbourne was typical of a great number of 'picture palaces' that were built in major cities, and sometimes in suburbs and country towns, throughout Australia during the 1920s. The interior is lavishly appointed and the stage area draped by sumptuous curtains. The huge organ to the left of the stage provided musical entertainment before the film and appropriately dramatic musical accompaniment during the screening. The boxes and the rather gaudy grandeur of the whole setting gave a visit to the cinema the air of a great theatrical occasion.

Melbourne's Capitol Theatre, which opened in 1924, was designed by Walter Burley Griffin and is distinguished by its magnificent ceiling in which coloured lights and shaped glass combine to produce spectacular and atmospheric effects.

Short skirts, low-slung waists and small hats that almost obscured the bobbed hairstyles all characterised the female fashions of the 1920s. These impeccably uniformed young women were some of the usherettes who showed people to their seats in Brisbane's Winter Garden Theatre.

In small picture houses in suburban and country venues a lone pianist often provided the supporting musical items and accompaniment. In the cities the various theatres vied with each other in their quest for musical spectacle and novelty. For many cinema patrons the theatrical environment and the musical trimmings were as important a part of a night out as the film being shown. This huge organ, being delivered with great ostentation to Adelaide's Regent Theatre in 1928, would no doubt have increased the theatre's patronage considerably.

Theatre interiors sometimes conjured up fantasies that rivalled or surpassed the illusions evoked by the flickering silver images on the screen. Often they reproduced, and usually with dubious authenticity, particular period styles. Sydney's Capitol Theatre was one of the more outlandish; with its star-studded domed ceiling, statues, arches and balustrades it sought to transport its patrons into an illusory ancient Roman setting.

Direct radio communication between Australia and Britain was established in the early 1920s under a controversial joint venture between the Hughes government and Amalgamated Wireless (Australasia) Ltd (generally known as AWA), under its dynamic and visionary managing director Ernest Fisk. The first direct radio message from England to Australia was sent in 1918, but the new agreement, signed in 1922, involved the setting up of new stations that would make for much cheaper communication than was available by means of existing cables. This photograph shows AWA's central radio office in Melbourne. Here messages in Morse were received, decoded, typed up and then delivered by messengers.

In 1923 the Victorian police became the first in the world to use mobile wireless receivers. This picture shows the first receiver, made by AWA Marconi, on the running board of a police car between the dog and W. R. Hutchinson, the first wireless operator. At first the machines were only able to receive, and not to transmit, messages. The man who later adapted the receiver for two-way communication, F. G. Canning, looks out from the back seat of the car.

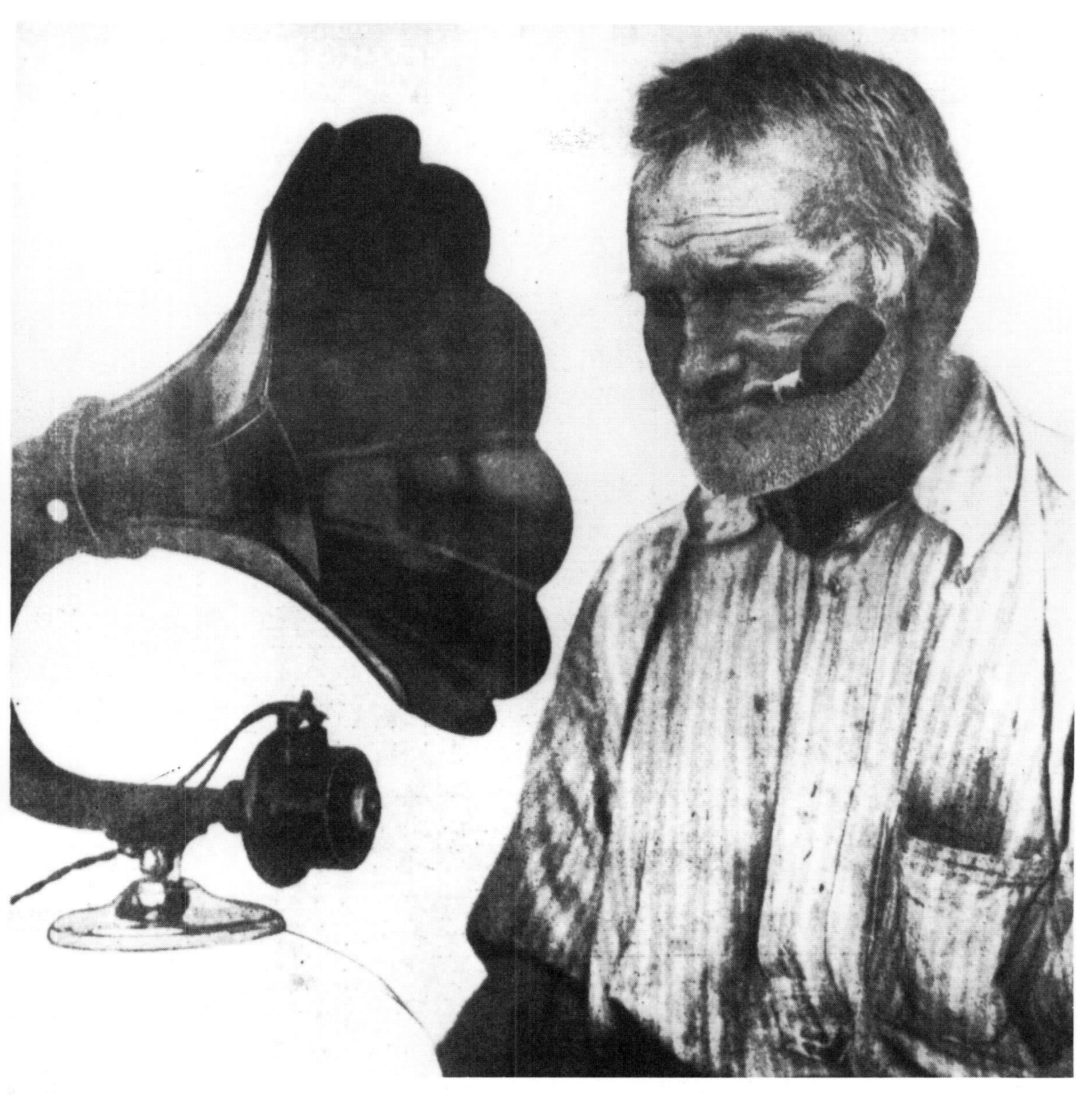

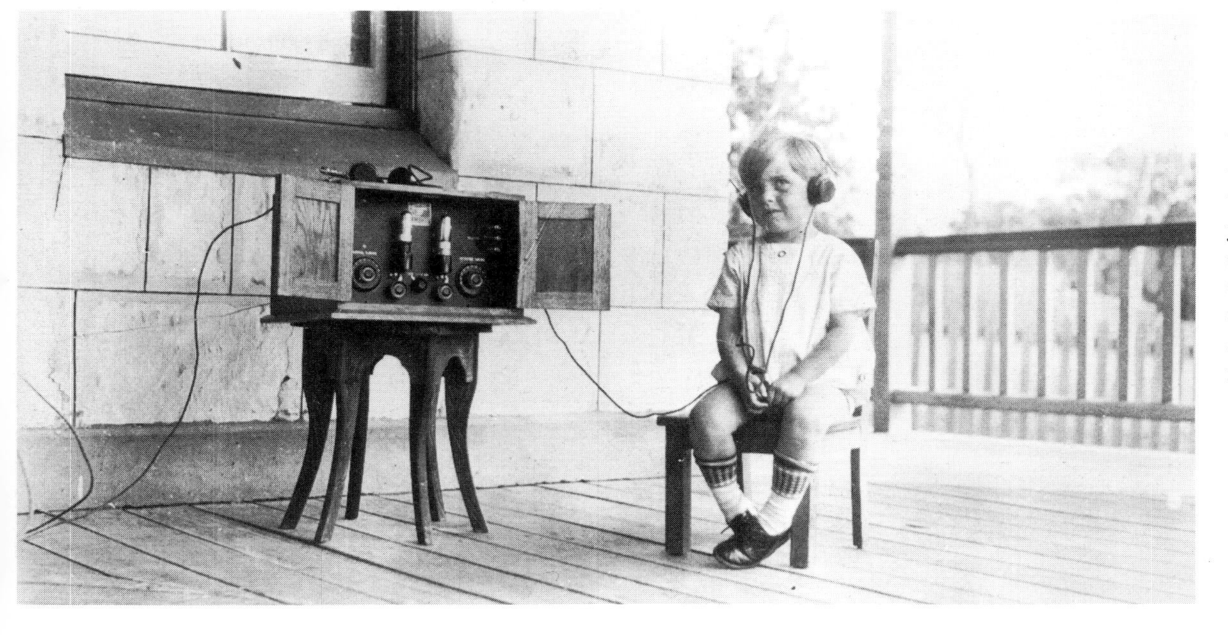

Wireless transmissions for domestic consumption began in 1923 when the first regular broadcasts were made in Sydney. At first listeners were obliged to subscribe to a particular station and all sets were 'sealed' so that they could only receive transmission from one station. In addition subscribers had to pay a licence fee of 10 shillings to the PMG's Department. General dissatisfaction with such an arrangement, as well as the ease with which the sets could be unsealed, forced the abandonment of this policy in 1924. By June 1924, there were two licensed stations in Sydney and one each in Melbourne and Perth.

Although public enthusiasm for the new phenomenon was high, the initial high cost of receivers and the limitations imposed by the sealed set system deterred people from investing in sets. After 1924, however, the wireless boomed as a form of home entertainment.

Reception from early home radio receivers was often unclear and subject to interference and static. In the above photo, published in the *Sun News-Pictorial* in 1925, this resident of an old persons' home in Melbourne stares with a kind of puzzled but tolerant amusement into the ungainly loudspeaker of the new machine that has just been purchased with a £100 bequest. The child (*bottom*) listens through earphones to a 'Mulgaphone', a West Australian receiver manufactured in 1924.

On Saturday 3 November 1923 serious rioting and looting broke out in Melbourne as a result of a police strike that left the streets virtually unprotected. Gangs roamed the city with impunity, smashing shop windows and provoking outbreaks of street fighting. A force of volunteer police or 'specials' were organised on the Sunday, and they managed to put down the violence and restore an uneasy calm.

Discontent in the police force had been brewing for some years but was brought to the boiling point by a change in disciplinary procedures that placed plain clothes constables in charge of uniformed police.

In the top photograph volunteers disperse a rioting mob by charging them with batons. In the bottom picture a group of specials arrive to quell a disturbance in Collins Street.

The stark effects of the riots of Saturday and Sunday, 3 and 4 November 1923. The smashed windows of these shops in Collins Street are boarded up to prevent further depredations.

In the second half of the 1920s industrial unrest was one of the major preoccupations of the Commonwealth government. Seamen and waterside workers were particularly militant and among their leaders were several British-born agitators, including Tom Walsh the president of the Australian Seamen's Union. In 1925 the government, using special legislation that had been brought in to deal with 'foreign agitators', tried to have Walsh deported for his part in a strike of British seamen. As he had lived in Australia since before World War I, however, the High Court disallowed the deportation order. Here, in Melbourne, British seamen march symbolically to prison during a strike for higher wages.

1985
SOUTHERN CROSS

Several pioneering feats of aviation fired the popular imagination and inspired large-scale displays of public enthusiasm during the 1920s. Perhaps the most important of these was the first aerial crossing of the Pacific Ocean — from San Francisco on the west coast of the United States, to Brisbane — by Charles Kingsford Smith and Charles Ulm. This photograph shows their three-engined Fokker F VIIb — the now legendary *Southern Cross* — arriving at Eagle Farm airport in Brisbane to a huge and excited reception after the 83-hour, 12 000-kilometre flight.

On 10 December 1919 Captain Ross Smith and his brother Keith landed their Vickers Vimy aircraft at Darwin and successfully concluded the first direct flight from England to Australia. By completing the journey within 30 days — with a mere two days to spare — the Smith brothers won themselves a prize of £10 000 that had been offered by the Commonwealth government and opened up the way for later commercial exploitation of the route. This photograph shows the welcome the Smiths received when they flew on to Sydney.

Just over eight years later, in February 1928, another historic landing was made at Darwin. This time Bert Hinkler completed the first solo England-to-Australia flight. On the ensuing tour of Australia, Hinkler was greeted by large crowds — like this one, which turned out in Perth. His Avro Avian biplane is in the background.

This Avro 504K (*top*) was one of the two World War I biplanes with which Hudson Fysh and Paul ('Ginty') McGuiness launched the operations of the Queensland and Northern Territory Aerial Services Ltd (QANTAS) in Longreach, Queensland, in 1920. These planes, which could carry a pilot and two passengers, undertook a number of excursion flights. In November 1922 QANTAS, with a subsidy from the Queensland government, began operating a regular service between Longreach and Cloncurry.

Another pioneer airline was the first Australian National Airways, formed in 1929 by Charles Kingsford Smith and Charles Ulm. Until financial troubles and the loss of one of its aircraft, the *Southern Cloud*, forced it to close down in 1931, this company operated regular services in Avro X aircraft, like the one pictured (*middle*), between Sydney and other capital cities. On 23 November 1931 the *Southern Sun* set out from Darwin on an airmail flight to England. It was wrecked three days later in an accident at Alor Setar in Malaya. Kingsford Smith set out in another aircraft, the *Southern Star*, collected the mail and flew it on to Britain, where it arrived before Christmas.

Flying was a hazardous business in aviation's early days. Ross Smith, Charles Kingsford Smith and Bert Hinkler were all killed in plane crashes, and the first attempt to fly the Tasman ended in tragedy. The sparse remains of this plane (*bottom*), which crashed in about 1927, dramatically illustrate the flimsiness of most early aircraft.

Women in the workforce during the 1920s were for the most part employed in repetitive and menial jobs. This picture shows women, standing in serried rows, cutting and stoning fruit in the Shepparton cannery in Victoria.

The increasing mechanisation of industry and the growth of mass production brought with it the drudgery of production-line work. In this photograph women work on conveyor belts at Arnott's biscuit factory in the Sydney suburb of Homebush.

During the 1920s many smaller-scale manufacturing enterprises were replaced by larger industrial complexes, which not only helped to change traditional work patterns but also brought heavy industry to many hitherto residential areas. This picture shows the Wellcome Australia pharmaceutical plant on the banks of the Parramatta River in the Sydney suburb of Mortlake.

The shorter skirts and looser garments — and even the short hair, which aroused the ire of sterner moral conservatives — that characterised the female fashions of the twenties allowed women a greater freedom of bodily movement. This was reflected in a corresponding increase in the sporting opportunities that were open to them. In the top picture, taken on the Gold Coast, the move, still incomplete, towards rational beachwear, can be seen.

The woman golfer (*bottom left*) and the young rowers (*bottom right*) could not have achieved the same ease of movement and feeling of relaxation in the clothes of a decade earlier.

In 1926 fierce bushfires raged through Gippsland in Victoria and 51 people lost their lives. The small sawmilling town of Noojee, at the foot of the Baw Baw Range, was destroyed in the inferno. The railway bridge, which had been built in 1919, remained precariously in place although several of its supports had been burnt through. The weight of these men was about as much as it could support. As a result of the 1926 fires, volunteer bushfire brigades were set up in Victoria in 1927 to try to avert further disasters. In 1939, however, in the devastating 'Black Friday' fires, Noojee once again fell victim to the flames.

The southern arm of the arch of the Sydney Harbour Bridge begins to reach out towards its northern counterpart in 1929. The splendour of the concept and the wonderful engineering feat that the bridge entailed probably meant little to the inhabitants of the depressed Rocks area of Sydney, where people lived in grinding poverty in dwellings that were for the most part cramped, run down and unhealthy. This photograph, by Harold Cazneaux, captures both the squalor of the slums and the incipient grandeur of the great arch.

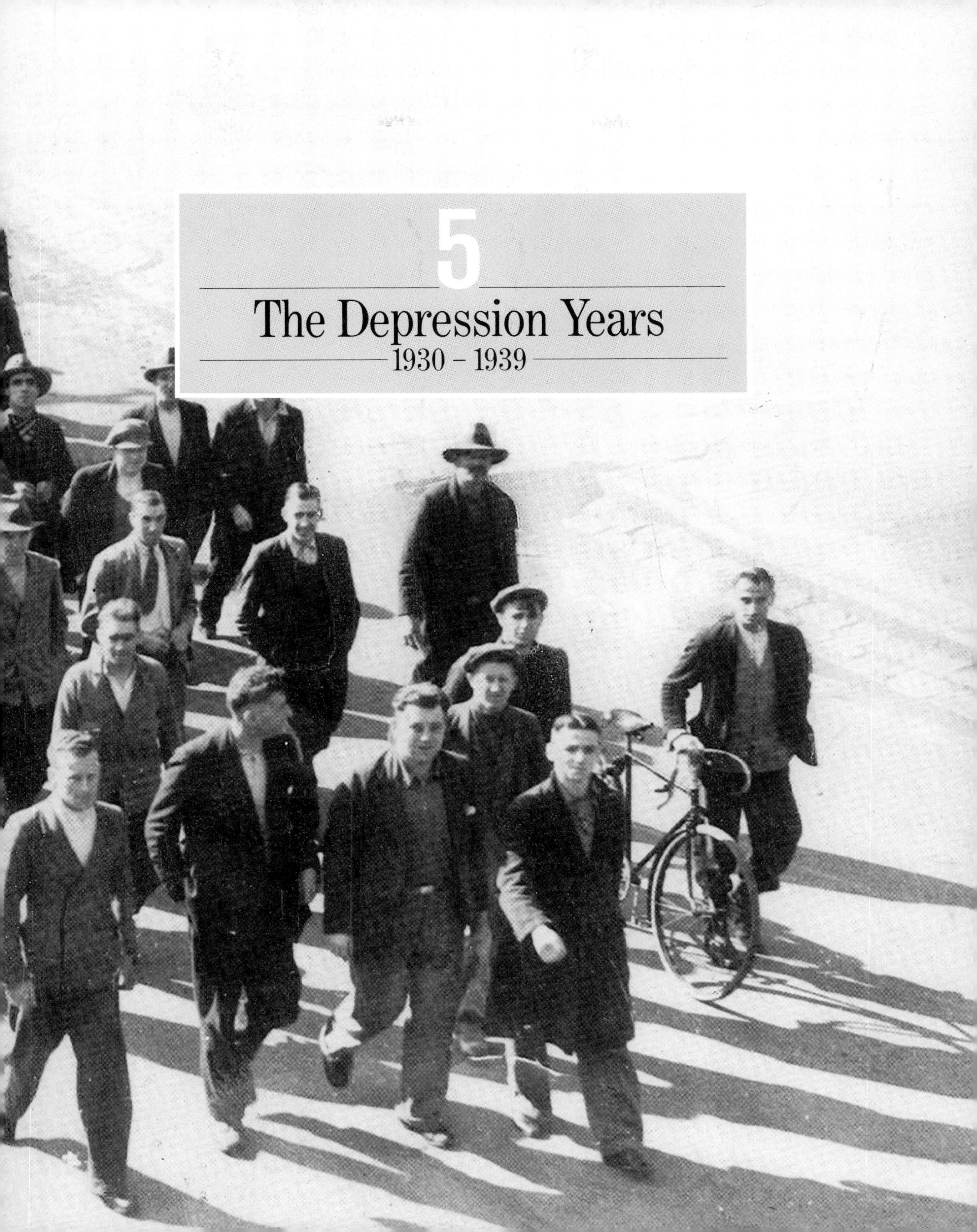

5
The Depression Years
1930 – 1939

The Depression took its toll on a wide cross-section of the Australian community, creating displacement, family dislocation, homelessness, hunger and mental and physical breakdown on an unprecedented scale. At the height of the crisis — in 1932 — almost one in three male breadwinners was out of work. The extent of deprivation can be gauged from the fact that female unemployment did not figure in the official statistics. Two years later the unemployment rate was still one in four. Even those who were fortunate enough to be in work found their real wages cut by 10 per cent as state and federal governments tried desperately to reduce the country's overseas debt.

The Depression left its trail of political casualties. It also inspired a polarisation of political forces, the formation of the ultra-right-wing paramilitary New Guard and the emergence of a new political party, the United Australia Party, as a result of defections from the Labor Party. The gathering economic gloom brought Labor under James Scullin to power in 1929 and left Stanley Bruce as the only Australian Prime Minister ever to be voted out of parliament. The worsening conditions brought about Scullin's resounding defeat in 1932. The most forthright and dominant politician of the era, the workers' champion Jack Lang, had his Premiership of New South Wales prematurely ended by viceregal intervention.

Conditions improved gradually after 1933 but unemployment mostly remained at pre-Depression levels for the rest of the decade. Politics became less volatile as unemployment fell. The United Australia Party, under the bland but widely accepted Joseph Lyons, retained power until Lyons' death in 1939.

As the decade came to a close and as war once again loomed, Robert Gordon Menzies emerged as the Prime Minister who would take Australia, behind Britain, into the fray.

Previous pages: Men on the move typified the Depression era. Armies of men, sometimes accompanied by their families, moved around the country in search of work or marched in protest against the conditions that had thrown them out of work.

Left: In 1939, when this photograph was taken at a Melbourne high society ball, the worst of the Depression was over, but the catastrophe of World War II was about to strike. No doubt the former had hardly affected these people and the likelihood of the latter had not yet impinged on them.

The Labor Prime Minister James Scullin (*top*), who came to office after the elections of October 1929, held the position for barely two years, during which his administration was wracked by internal wrangling and beset by seemingly insuperable economic difficulties. Scullin's famed oratorical skills were of little avail in the turbulent and volatile political atmosphere of the time.

Although Scullin has sometimes been characterised as a weak leader, he overcame strong opposition in two areas that affected Australia's independence. He managed to argue successfully for the immunity of Australian legislation from British interference and, in face of strong objections from King George V, he insisted on the appointment of Sir Isaac Isaacs — pictured (*bottom right*) with Lady Isaacs — as the first Australian-born Governor-General. The conservative British opposition to an Australian appointment was all the stronger because of the nominee's Jewishness.

Joseph Lyons, pictured (*bottom left*) with British Prime Minister Stanley Baldwin, was Postmaster-General in Scullin's government. His defection to the conservatives with four other ministers was instrumental in precipitating the collapse of the government. He became leader of the newly formed United Australia Party, which resoundingly won the elections of December 1931, and remained Prime Minister until his death in 1939.

Jack Lang, nicknamed the 'Big Fella', was twice Labor Premier of New South Wales — from 1925 to 1927 and, during the period of federal Labor rule, from 1930 to 1932. The most forceful Australian politician of his day, he inspired both great loyalty and virulent hatred. Seen here addressing a rally of supporters, Lang, like Scullin, was an effective speaker, but with a hectoring belligerent manner that reflected his general political style.

Lang earned the enmity of conservatives by his vigorous support of the rights of the working classes, whom he believed were being required, even by the federal Labor government, to bear the brunt of the economic crisis. He publicly attacked the 'Premiers' Plan', which was adopted in 1931 and which would effectively cut workers' real wages, and pressed for Australia to freeze, if not entirely abandon, the repayment of its British debts. Such an anti-British stand was anathema to many Australians. It was Lang's attempt to implement this policy by refusing to hand over state revenues to the Commonwealth that led the state Governor, Sir Philip Game, to dismiss him from office in May 1932. In the subsequent elections, Labor was comprehensively, and predictably, defeated.

ENGELS
OLD VIENNA

The real or imagined threat of communism was heavily exploited by the opponents of Labor in the early thirties. The flaunting at May Day marches of banners, like these ones by the artist Noel Counihan, showing heroes of the Russian Revolution, could only have further incensed anti-Labor feeling and increased public support for a number of right-wing paramilitary organisations that sprang up at the time.

It is ironic that the most enduring symbol of Australia's largest city, the Sydney Harbour Bridge, begun nine years earlier in a climate of optimism, should have been opened at a time of economic crisis and national despondency. The progress of the two arms of the great arch provided Sydneysiders during 1929 and 1930 with a continuing spectacle, and a subject for speculation: would they meet in the middle? The top photograph shows the arms close to joining in July 1930.

The most prominent and vociferous of the extreme right-wing groups that flourished briefly in the early thirties was the New Guard, which was formed in New South Wales with the express purpose of hounding Lang from office, and which espoused such popular loyalist causes as absolute allegiance to the British monarchy and Empire and a determination to exterminate communism.

The New Guard seized the limelight at the opening ceremony of the Sydney Harbour Bridge on 19 March 1932, when a Captain de Groot (*bottom left*) rode up on horseback and slashed the ribbon in order to prevent the 'unworthy' Lang from performing the ceremony. Captain de Groot was arrested and removed from the scene, the ribbon was rejoined and the Premier proceeded as planned (*bottom right*).

Crowds stream across the bridge immediately after the disrupted opening ceremony, taking advantage of an opportunity to view the city and harbour from an entirely new perspective. Three days earlier 50 000 schoolchildren had been allowed to walk across the bridge. It would not be until the 1982 anniversary of the opening that pedestrians would once again have access to the roadway.

Of all the colonies Western Australia had been the most reluctant to join the new Commonwealth. Its geographic isolation and the tariff policies that West Australians thought discriminated against their interests kept secessionist sentiments to the fore. In 1932, the worst year of the Depression, the state government held a referendum in which voters decided, by almost two to one, to secede. Both the Commonwealth and the British governments rejected the state's appeal to form a separate dominion and the idea eventually lapsed. The picture shows the grand banquet held in the Perth Town Hall to celebrate the result of the referendum.

STRALIA
HALL BE
TREE

As unemployment worsened during 1930 and 1931 evictions for non-payment of rent became common, especially in Melbourne and Sydney. The victims did not always accept quietly the prospect of homelessness. Pickets were organised outside the homes of people who were to be turned out and police often forcibly removed the entrenched tenants. In one incident at Newtown in Sydney, in June 1931, a bloody battle between police and pickets resulted in 27 casualties. Just a month later, in Melbourne, an angry mob destroyed a house from which a woman and her children had been evicted.

Many of the homeless drifted to the miserable shanty settlements that grew up at Dudley Flats in Melbourne and La Perouse in Sydney. The top photograph, taken in 1938, shows the collection of makeshift dwellings that were still occupied at Dudley Flats, even after the worst times were over. In the bottom photograph, taken in 1936, a man, obviously acclimatised to his reduced state, takes the air outside his crude shack. The sheet of galvanised iron that forms the roof is held in place only by the weight of the stones that are piled on top.

In Adelaide during 1930 this collection of huts, tents and humpies grew up along the bank of the Torrens, only to be swept away the next year when the river flooded.

Dressed with the shabby formality that characterised the dispossessed of the thirties, these men, forcing smiles for the sake of the camera, have assembled to receive a handout of meat at West Perth during 1930. Not far away, at East Perth, a special outdoor butchery had been set up to provide free meat for those who could not afford to buy it.

The plight of the poor made good human interest material for newspapers during the 1930s and provided news photographers with a ready source of subjects. The photographs on this and the next page, taken in the working class Melbourne suburb of Richmond, appeared in Melbourne newspapers in 1936 and 1937. The social conventions of the time meant that men, even when thrown into idleness by lack of employment, still took little responsibility for the maintenance of domestic order or for the care of children. Women were expected to cook, clean and generally keep up the tone of a household with ever-dwindling resources. Many, in areas like Richmond, took over the role of breadwinner as well as housekeeper, by taking in washing or doing housework for more affluent people.

This mother of seven, prematurely aged by hardship and deprivation, boils up the washing in two old kerosene tins over a fuel stove. Quite possibly the kerosene tins would have doubled as cooking utensils.

The experience of living in conditions like these and the certainty that there was no relief in sight brought a range of reactions from different women and their families. Some succumbed to despondency and allowed their standards of dress and cleanliness to degenerate; others maintained their meagre possessions with scrupulous care. In the top picture four children and the family pet can be seen in their back yard, while another two children peer curiously through the window — the young girl gazing wistfully at the camera is probably holding her youngest sibling. The appearance of the children suggests that the family is coping despite shabby surroundings. The expression and stance of the woman in the bottom picture, standing disconsolately next to the corrugated iron outhouse that serves as bathroom and toilet, imply a pent-up frustration that is close to breaking point.

Destitution caused many people to live in the open or to take refuge in such natural shelters as the sandstone caves in Sydney's Domain. The man in the top picture, boiling a billy on an improvised stove, will later bed down on the park bench. The young man (*bottom*) has shown considerable resourcefulness in fitting out his 'home' and is now effecting some essential repairs to his already threadbare trousers.

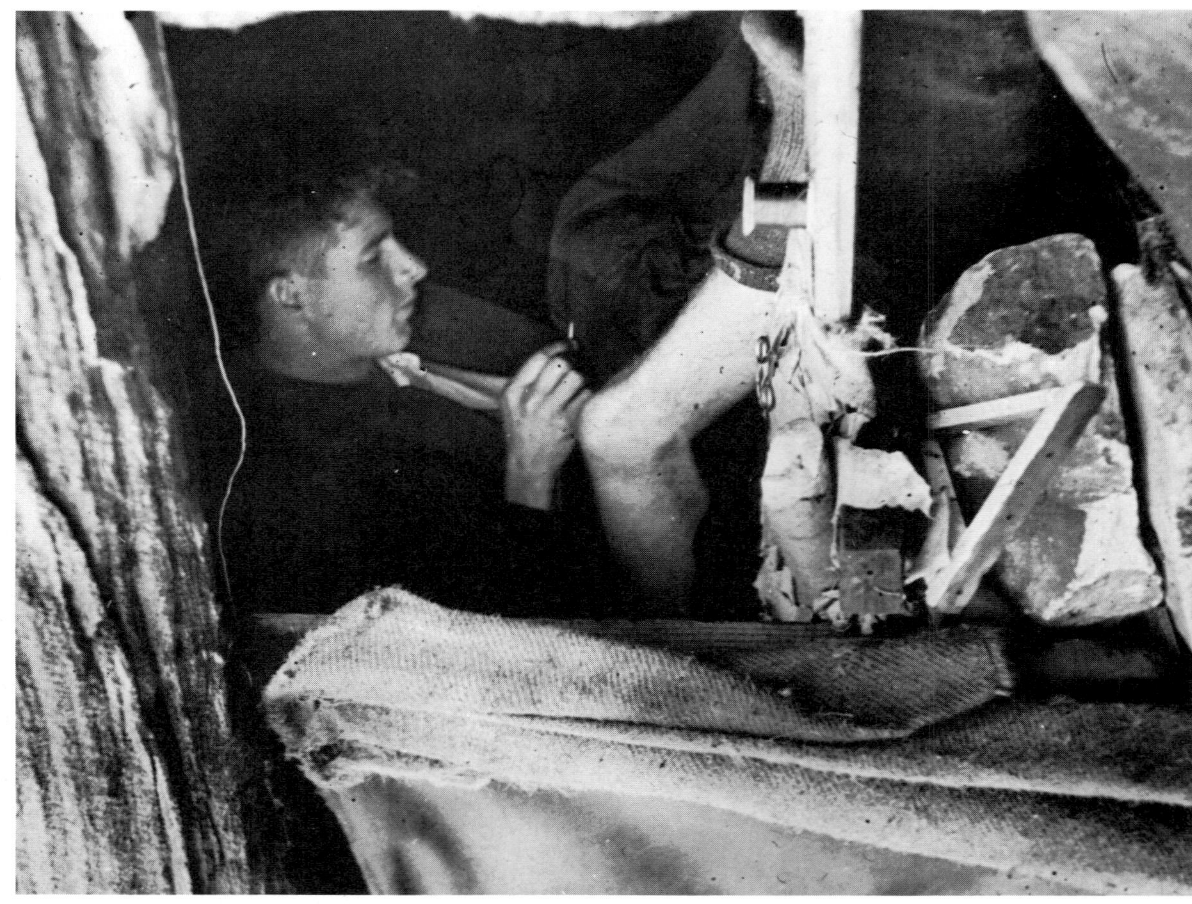

The business of looking for work could be both dangerous and expensive and would-be workers often found themselves in a vicious circle. The widespread practice of jumping on moving goods trains — 'jumping the rattler', it was called — in order to get to new places in search of work could mean instant death, or a prison sentence. Tramping the city or countryside in search of work took its inevitable toll on boot-leather and brought in no money with which to buy new footwear. Advertising one's availability by means of a sandwich board was more likely to inspire hostility than job offers and was probably more indicative of desperation than of hope.

One form of work made available to unemployed men, at first by local and state governments and after 1934 by the federal government, was relief work. Government and civic projects were often carried out using this form of conscripted labour. Instead of receiving unemployment relief, men were required to work, sometimes for only two or three days a week, on building roads, monuments, or on agricultural projects, sometimes in remote and inhospitable places. For this they were paid much less than a normal working wage and very little more than the unemployment relief, which they would forgo if they refused the relief job.

This portrait of a relief worker reflects the desperate state to which many men had been reduced. Without adequate clothing, and with his feet dangerously exposed, he works for a pittance digging trenches.

Incongruously dressed in the remnants of their suits and waistcoats, these relief workers — sometimes referred to as 'sussos' — are building the Yarra Boulevard in Melbourne. Melbourne's Shrine of Remembrance was also built using relief workers.

City men were often required to leave their families to undertake relief jobs in country areas. In many cases they were accommodated in camps, such as this one in Western Australia, where poor sanitation and inadequate protection from rain and cold made them an easy prey to illness and infection. Morale was understandably low among relief workers, and strikes about their conditions of work were very frequent. The system was also exploited by some unscrupulous employers who sacked their regular workers in order to take advantage of the much cheaper rates paid to relief workers.

One of the most famous images of the Depression, this photograph shows an ocean of felt-hatted men queuing at specially erected barricades at Sydney's Circular Quay to collect their relief coupons. With true bureaucratic insensitivity, the authorities decided to make the food that the coupons could procure available near Central Railway at the other end of the city. The men could either walk the several kilometres or spend their meagre savings on a tram fare. The men at the front of the queue are preparing to present their relief cards to the officials who are handing out the coupons. The card contained what amounted to a declaration of destitution on the part of the holder and the date and value of each handout was clearly entered. Not surprisingly, attempts to cheat the system were frequent.

For those women who could afford to wear the latest fashions, longer skirts, more tightly fitting garments and wide-brimmed hats had, by the late thirties, replaced the loose and leggy look of the twenties. Formal wear often featured daringly low necklines and backs. These Adelaide women are doing Christmas shopping in 1938.

Several times violent storms destroyed the flimsy dwellings that the unemployed had built themselves on the fringes of the capital cities. In June 1931 a gale, accompanied by torrential rain, blew and washed away tents and huts at Sydney's Happy Valley settlement. In September of the same year the River Torrens flooded in Adelaide, submerging the huts in this settlement and subjecting the already destitute to even further deprivation.

In late 1934 Australia experienced severe and widespread flooding. Parts of New South Wales, Queensland, South Australia and Western Australia were hit, but the worst disaster occurred in Victoria where Gippsland and the Yarra Valley were inundated. The ordeal began on 29 November when the Yarra broke its bank and parts of Melbourne were submerged. In all 35 people lost their lives and about £1.5 million worth of damage was done. The Burke Road bridge was under water for several days. In this photograph police wade waist deep through waters covering Kaidoura Avenue, Hawthorn, to help stranded residents.

The pictures on this page graphically depict the destruction wrought by the bushfires that laid waste vast areas of Victoria in January 1939 and that reached their terrible culmination on 'Black Friday', the thirteenth. The country had suffered a long period of drought and there had been outbreaks of fire during the spring and early summer. Heatwave conditions and high winds whipped up the flames of a number of fires that had been burning separately and turned them into one great conflagration, which roared relentlessly across the state, killing 71 people, destroying more than a thousand homes and burning 2 million hectares of countryside. In the heavily timbered regions 69 sawmills were destroyed. The top picture shows the site of the destroyed Rubicon mill where seven lives were lost. In the gruesome bottom photograph bodies are being retrieved from a mill near the town of Alexandra.

Sport provided some distraction from the troubles of the time and internationally successful sportsmen, perhaps more than achievers in any other field, gave people a sense of national pride. Cricket Test series between Australia and England were major international events and much of the submerged hostility that existed in relations between the countries erupted in these matches. The 1932-33 English tour of Australia was marked by great bitterness, caused by a new bowling technique espoused by the English team. The English called it, innocuously enough, 'leg theory'. It became universally known as 'bodyline' because it involved bowling fast high-bouncing deliveries directly at the batsman. Australian indignation was inflamed by incidents such as the one in the top photograph in which the Australian batsman Bert Oldfield falls to the ground after being struck on the head by a ball from the English bowler Harold Larwood.

The public interest that cricket aroused can be gauged by the keenness with which the large crowd (*bottom*) inspects the wicket before the Melbourne Test in the 1936-37 Test series.

The reason for the invention of bodyline bowling was probably the emergence of Don Bradman, the greatest batsman in the history of cricket, at the end of the 1920s. From 1936 until 1948 Bradman was the captain of the Australian team and under his leadership Australia did not lose a series. He is shown (*top left*) executing a hook shot during the 1936-37 series against England.

Another Australian sporting hero of the 1930s was Hugh Opperman (*top right*), perhaps the world's greatest long-distance cyclist for most of the 1920s and 1930s. Opperman retired from competitive cycling in 1940, and later achieved national prominence as a politician and member of several Menzies ministries.

By the 1930s Australian beaches had become the playgrounds of the young and energetic and surfing had become one of the most popular summer pastimes. In 1930 there were almost 90 surf lifesaving clubs operating on Australian beaches. These young lifesavers (*bottom*) are training at Henley Beach, South Australia in 1938.

1938

The 1930s also saw the beaches of Queensland's Gold Coast — it would not be so named until 1958 — emerge as a tourist attraction. This novel composition, taken by the Tweed Heads photographer, Fred Lang, in 1938, gives a good idea of the range of swimwear available and the degree of undress that was tolerated by this time.

The defunct Australian film industry was resurrected in 1931 with the formation of two companies — Cinesound Productions in Sydney and Efftee Films in Melbourne — that were to produce a succession of talking films throughout the decade. Many of their films were box-office successes in Australia and several were sold and shown in England. The vaudeville comedian, George Wallace, was able to make the transition from stage to screen and starred in films made by both companies. He is seen here casting amorous glances at Gwen Munro in the 1938 Cinesound film *Let George Do It*.

One of the most popular Australian entertainers, who also achieved fame and fortune overseas, was the South Australian born baritone, Peter Dawson. Dawson, though best known as a singer of popular ballads, was also a concert and operatic singer. He was a prolific recording artist; his recordings number about 3500. In this photograph, taken in the BBC studios in London, he is both recording and making a live broadcast.

The unmistakable profile of Australia's greatest clown, Roy Rene 'Mo'. During his long career on stage and radio, which extended for almost forty years, 'Mo' delighted generations of Australians, and offended quite a few, with his idiosyncratic and often vulgarly suggestive humour. He began his career as a vaudeville artist as part of the team of 'Stiffy and Mo'. Despite his enormous popularity his one foray onto the screen, in the Cinesound feature *Strike Me Lucky* — named after one of the many sayings that Mo bequeathed to the Australian language — was a failure.

The sleek blue and golden lines, high speed and air-conditioned comfort of the handsome new *Spirit of Progress*, pictured (*bottom*) after it had been 'christened' by the Victorian Premier, Mr Dunstan, in November 1939, presented a strong contrast to the many more archaic forms of transport still being used in Melbourne and other Australian cities. Even in the late 1930s the horse-drawn wagon was still the most common means of delivering goods to markets, and bread, ice and milk to homes.

The *Spirit of Progress* was to be for many years Australia's most luxurious and fastest train. It was Australia's first air-conditioned train and the first Australian train to be built entirely of steel. In terms that anticipated later attempts to promote public transport, the Victorian Premier depicted the train as a way of meeting 'the challenge of the road'. 'The association of speed and comfort,' he added, 'will persuade the public to use the railways more.' Unfortunately, the *Spirit of Progress* had to end its journey at the Victorian border. The difference in gauge meant that passengers had to transfer to a much less comfortable New South Wales train to complete the trip to Sydney.

A horse-drawn cab in Sydney in 1935. The cab, already archaic, would soon disappear from Sydney streets. The building it is approaching — the historic and beautiful Royal Exchange, on the corner of Pitt and Bridge streets and then just over 80 years old — would survive for another thirty years before it succumbed to the redevelopment craze of the sixties.

The pedal radio was to transform the lives of remote outback dwellers by putting them in direct communication with others in distant places. It was also to be the instrument for saving lives: the pedal radio made possible the development of Australia's Flying Doctor Service. The pedal radio was developed by an Adelaide electrical engineer, Alfred Traeger, at the instigation of the Reverend J. Flynn, who in 1927 founded the Flying Doctor Service. The earliest pedal radios, like the one being used by the Reverend Skipper Partridge in 1930 (*bottom*), transmitted messages in Morse. By 1932 Traeger had refined this by the addition of a keyboard that would allow typed-out messages to be transmitted in Morse, and in 1935 direct voice contact became possible. This meant that people like Mrs Irene Fuller, pictured (*top*) in 1938 at Newry station in the Northern Territory could speak directly to the Flying Doctor Service in Wyndham, Western Australia, could explain matters such as symptoms and could receive advice about what to do until help arrived.

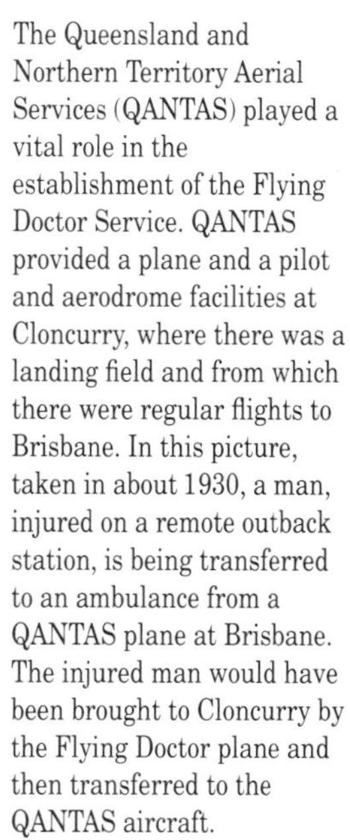

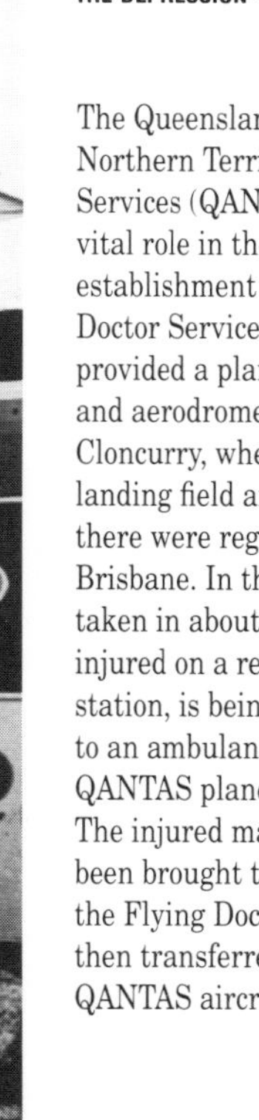

The Queensland and Northern Territory Aerial Services (QANTAS) played a vital role in the establishment of the Flying Doctor Service. QANTAS provided a plane and a pilot and aerodrome facilities at Cloncurry, where there was a landing field and from which there were regular flights to Brisbane. In this picture, taken in about 1930, a man, injured on a remote outback station, is being transferred to an ambulance from a QANTAS plane at Brisbane. The injured man would have been brought to Cloncurry by the Flying Doctor plane and then transferred to the QANTAS aircraft.

On 23 April 1931 the first experimental air mail from Australia to England left Melbourne. It was flown out of Darwin to Akyab in Burma by Kingsford Smith on 27 April, where it was handed over to Imperial Airways and then flown on to London. This photograph shows the mail ready to be loaded on to the plane in Melbourne. At the extreme left is Hudson Fysh, one of the founders of QANTAS.

In the 1920s and 1930s many affluent households found it difficult to find domestic servants. One source of cheap and supposedly pliable domestic help were young Aboriginal women, most of them hardly more than children, who were forcibly recruited from reserves and missions and put to work as domestics. A number of institutions were established to provide a short period of basic training before the girls were assigned to their employers. The practice was justified on the grounds that this was a form of Aboriginal education. Many of the girls were not paid for their service and many absconded before their term of 'apprenticeship' was finished. These young domestic trainees were photographed at Cootamundra Home, run by the New South Wales Aboriginal Protection Board, in about 1930.

Early in 1934 the Victorian government coal mine at Wonthaggi, the source of coal for Victoria's railways, was shut down in an extended showdown between miners and the Department of Railways. The immediate cause was an attempt to cut mine wages by much more than the 10 per cent that most workers had accepted. The miners and the rest of the town displayed a remarkable solidarity by virtually living off the natural resources of the surrounding countryside, and the ocean, for several months, thus indicating that the mine needed the miners more than the miners needed the mine. In June the authorities were eventually forced to capitulate. During the dispute the women of the town organised themselves into an auxiliary, shown here marching in a protest procession. The auxiliary collected money, organised the distribution of goods and publicised the miners' cause in other parts of the country.

Late in 1938 a dispute arose about the export of Australian pig-iron to Japan. Japan's aggression against China had stirred fears of possible Japanese expansionist intentions. When pig-iron intended for Japan began to pile up on Port Kembla wharves the Attorney-General, R. G. Menzies, forced the waterside workers to load it by threatening legal action against them. The threat earned Menzies the enduring nickname 'Pig-Iron Bob'.

Despite the increasing tension in relations between Britain — and therefore by implication Australia — and Germany, large growds turned out in Brisbane to welcome a group of visiting German athletes in the late 1930s. Here, bearing swastikas and a banner declaring them, in typical Nazi propagandist style, to be 'Young, Godly, Happy and Free', the athletes parade through the city.

As war became more imminent some people began to take precautions. This group, photographed in 1938, is practising the art of survival in the presence of noxious gases.

The public consciousness of impending war was also raised by a greater conspicuousness of men in uniform at public events. These members of the Light Horse gave a demonstration of their skills at Sydney's Royal Agricultural and Horticultural Society show in 1938.

6
The World War II Years
1939 – 1949

After an initially apathetic response to the war in Europe, characterised by the government's low-key 'business as usual' policy and by a lack of public commitment to recruitment, Australians were jolted into a state of alarm by Japan's spectacular entry into the war and by its assumed ambition to occupy Australia. A fear of Asia, a result of the country's deeply felt isolation from the roots of its European culture — repeatedly expressed in its determination to maintain its racial homogeneity — made the idea of Japanese invasion and rule doubly repugnant to Australians. The violation of Australian territory by the air strikes against Darwin and other parts of northern Australia, the infiltration of Sydney Harbour by Japanese submarines and the shelling from off the coast of parts of Sydney and Newcastle gave Australian civilians their first and terrifying direct experience of warfare.

The threat was real and was perceived to be so, and it prompted the Labor Prime Minister, John Curtin, to take the courageous and unprecedented step of recalling Australian troops, despite British displeasure at the move, to defend Australia. It even enabled him, in the face of strong anti-conscription feeling in the community and the Labor Party, to obtain approval for the deployment of conscripted Australian troops in a limited area outside Australian territory.

At home the war acted as a liberating force, if only a temporary one, for many women who entered the paid workforce to replace men on active service. Women's contribution to the war effort, too, went far beyond the role that had traditionally been expected of them. Their support in conventional ways was as forthcoming as ever, but there was a desire, at first resisted and sometimes ridiculed, for active involvement that resulted in a rash of women's military groups and led to the participation of large numbers of women in the armed forces.

Significant and lasting reforms were achieved during the period of Labor government that began in 1941 and lasted until 1949. Unashamedly socialist in its aims, Chifley's post-war government, in particular, enacted controversial but now well accepted reforms in the areas of banking and social welfare; it nationalised QANTAS, set up a national domestic airline, established the Australian National University in Canberra, and espoused the ideal of full employment. Perhaps its most lasting and far-reaching legacy was the launching of Australia's ambitious post-war immigration scheme.

Previous pages: Twenty-one years after the cessation of hostilities in World War I, Australia was again at war and the country's able-bodied young men were embarking for service in distant foreign parts. As before, women were left to maintain homes, support the war effort and keep industries going while expectantly and anxiously awaiting their men's return.

Left: Though war in Europe was, in retrospect at least, clearly imminent, and Australia's involvement in that war would be an automatic consequence of Britain's entry, almost no preparations were underway when the declaration was made. Here, in early 1939, a member of Australia's 80 000-strong voluntary militia handles an obsolete means of transporting obsolete equipment, much of it the out-of-date remnants of the previous war.

A truck bearing a none-too-subtle message is driven through Melbourne during a procession in 1942. The two great 'isms' of the war — Nazism and Fascism — meant little to most Australians, for the war was, at first, simply a matter of 'stopping Hitler', a feat that, it was generally assumed, would be quickly and efficiently achieved. By the time this photograph was taken, however, such ideologies were even less relevant. Japan had entered the war and Australians were desperately preoccupied with their own survival.

These volunteers for the Second AIF are given a rowdy farewell as they leave Melbourne in January 1940 to embark for the Middle East. Their train is garishly emblazoned with morale-boosting graffiti, including swastikas, slogans and caricatures of Hitler.

Despite Menzies' early declaration that Australia was at war, the government, supported by the opposition, was at first disinclined to commit troops overseas. Having made Australia's support for Britain clear, Menzies proceeded to play things down by declaring a policy of 'business as usual'. A threat from Japan was thought to be a real possibility and the government considered that Australia's best immediate course was to secure its own defences. A storm of protest from Empire loyalists prompted a rapid about face. Less than two weeks after declaring war, Menzies announced in a broadcast that a special force of 20 000 men would be recruited to serve, presumably in Europe. This force was recruited, despite a disconcerting reluctance among members of the voluntary militia to offer themselves for overseas service, by the end of 1939. In January 1940 the first troops, members of the 6th Division, sailed from Sydney.

Their departure was officially a secret. A newspaper cartoon, however, alerted the public to the impending departure and thousands lined Sydney Harbour to gain a view of the departing troops.

Australians took to heart Menzies' exhortation to conduct business as usual. Their casual reaction to the war was reflected in the initial slowness of men to enlist. Two months after recruiting began men were still being sought to fill the special overseas force of 20 000, despite a lowering of the required standards of fitness. The rush of volunteers that had overwhelmed recruiting offices in 1914, and that was confidently expected in 1939, failed to eventuate. Active campaigning had to be resorted to and prominent citizens were called upon to bring their influence to bear. Here Gladys Moncrief — 'Our Glad', Australia's great operetta and musical comedy star of the twenties and thirties — stands on a gun carriage to address a recruiting rally in Melbourne.

While attempts to recruit men into the services met with only a lukewarm response, a range of unofficial women's military and paramilitary groups sprang up, many of them with their own distinctive uniforms. Some groups attended regular drill sessions and were trained in the use of weapons. An attempt to coordinate these disparate organisations was made in New South Wales, with the keen cooperation of the state government but without a corresponding enthusiasm from the federal government. About 10 000 women attended a meeting in the Sydney Town Hall to inaugurate the Women's Australian National Service (WANS), which was formed under the patronage of Lady Wakehurst, wife of the state Governor. Women trained in different branches of the services and acquired a variety of specialised skills in which they were required to pass tests.

In 1941 officially sanctioned women's branches of all the services were formed. In the top photograph members of the Women's Royal Australian Naval Service (WRANS) are seen at drill in Sydney. The bottom photograph shows a member of the Australian Women's Army Service (AWAS) at rifle practice near Perth in May 1943.

The entry of Italy into the war on 10 June 1940 meant that the Mediterranean became the main theatre of naval action and the scene of the first important naval engagements. The Australian cruiser HMAS *Sydney* arrived in the Mediterranean in May 1940. On 19 July it took part, in conjunction with five British destroyers, in an engagement with two Italian cruisers. The *Sydney* sank one of the Italian ships, the *Bartolomeo Colleoni*. In this photograph, taken from the deck of the *Sydney*, the *Bartolomeo Colleoni* is seen in flames after the encounter.

One of the most renowned campaigns in which Australians took part was the siege of Tobruk, a rugged seaport in Libya. Four Australian infantry brigades formed part of 31 000 Allied troops that occupied the town after the fall of the Italian garrison there in January 1941. In April, German and Italian troops surrounded Tobruk, thus beginning a siege that lasted 242 days until the Axis troops were finally forced to withdraw on 10 December. The defenders, who were nicknamed the 'Rats of Tobruk', dug in behind barbed-wire defences. Most of the Australians were evacuated under cover of night before the siege had ended. This photograph shows a burial party outside the town.

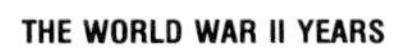

Australian troops, inside Tobruk after the Italian surrender in January 1941, organise an impromptu cricket game amid the dust and rubble, while one of their number keeps a lookout for enemy aircraft from a balcony.

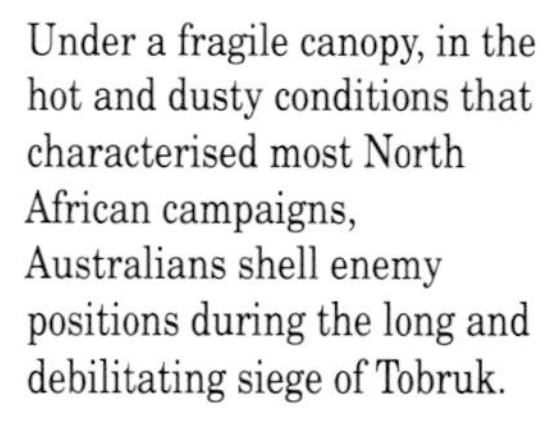

Under a fragile canopy, in the hot and dusty conditions that characterised most North African campaigns, Australians shell enemy positions during the long and debilitating siege of Tobruk.

In late 1941, as a result of long-brewing dissensions within the United Australia Party, Menzies resigned as Prime Minister. Some weeks later the government, now led by Arthur Fadden, was defeated in a confidence motion and Labor, under John Curtin, came to office. Curtin, in contrast to the aloof and sometimes haughty Menzies, was a simple, unpretentious and serious man who, as a wartime leader, won the respect both of colleagues and opponents. He made a close friend of Ray Tracey (on the right), his official chauffeur, who became a frequent visitor to the Lodge, where this photograph of the two men was taken.

The attack on Pearl Harbor by the Japanese caused Curtin to reassess Australia's war priorities. At the end of 1941 he had already made what to some was the heretical statement that Australia must look to the United States rather than to Britain for defence. In February 1942, after the fall of Singapore, Curtin asked that two of the three Australian divisions in the Middle East be returned to Australia. Churchill ordered that they be sent instead to Burma, but this order was countermanded by Curtin. For the first time Australia as a nation had put her own interests before those of the 'mother country'. The troops arrived back in March to a tumultuous welcome from a now frightened populace. In this photograph returning troops are showered with streamers and papers in George Street, Sydney.

In what the *Sydney Morning Herald* portentously described as 'the opening shots in the Battle of Australia' the totally unprepared city of Darwin was twice ravaged by Japanese bombers on the morning of 19 February 1942, just four days after the fall of Singapore. The first raid, at about 10 a.m., attacked the town and ships in the harbour, and the second, two hours later, attacked the airfield. Australian and United States ships and planes were destroyed, 243 people were killed and hundreds more injured, and much of the town was reduced to rubble.

In an effort to play down the severity of the attacks and to allay panic about an imminent invasion the official death toll was placed, and maintained, at eleven. In fact, these raids, and more than sixty others that followed, were not part of an invasion plan, but an attempt to neutralise Darwin as a base from which the planned invasion of Port Moresby could be thwarted.

In this picture firefighters shelter behind an asbestos shield as they train water on blazing storage tanks.

The destruction of this hangar at Darwin's airfield gives an impression of the savage destruction achieved by the Japanese raids.

This elderly soldier was a member of the Volunteer Defence Corps, a group of World War I veterans (affectionately nicknamed 'retreads'), which was formed in mid-1940 and which, by dint of sheer persistence, was granted rather begrudging government support and approval to perform home duties and undertake defence in the event of an invasion. In fact, government support turned out to be more token than real; many members were never issued with uniforms or weapons.

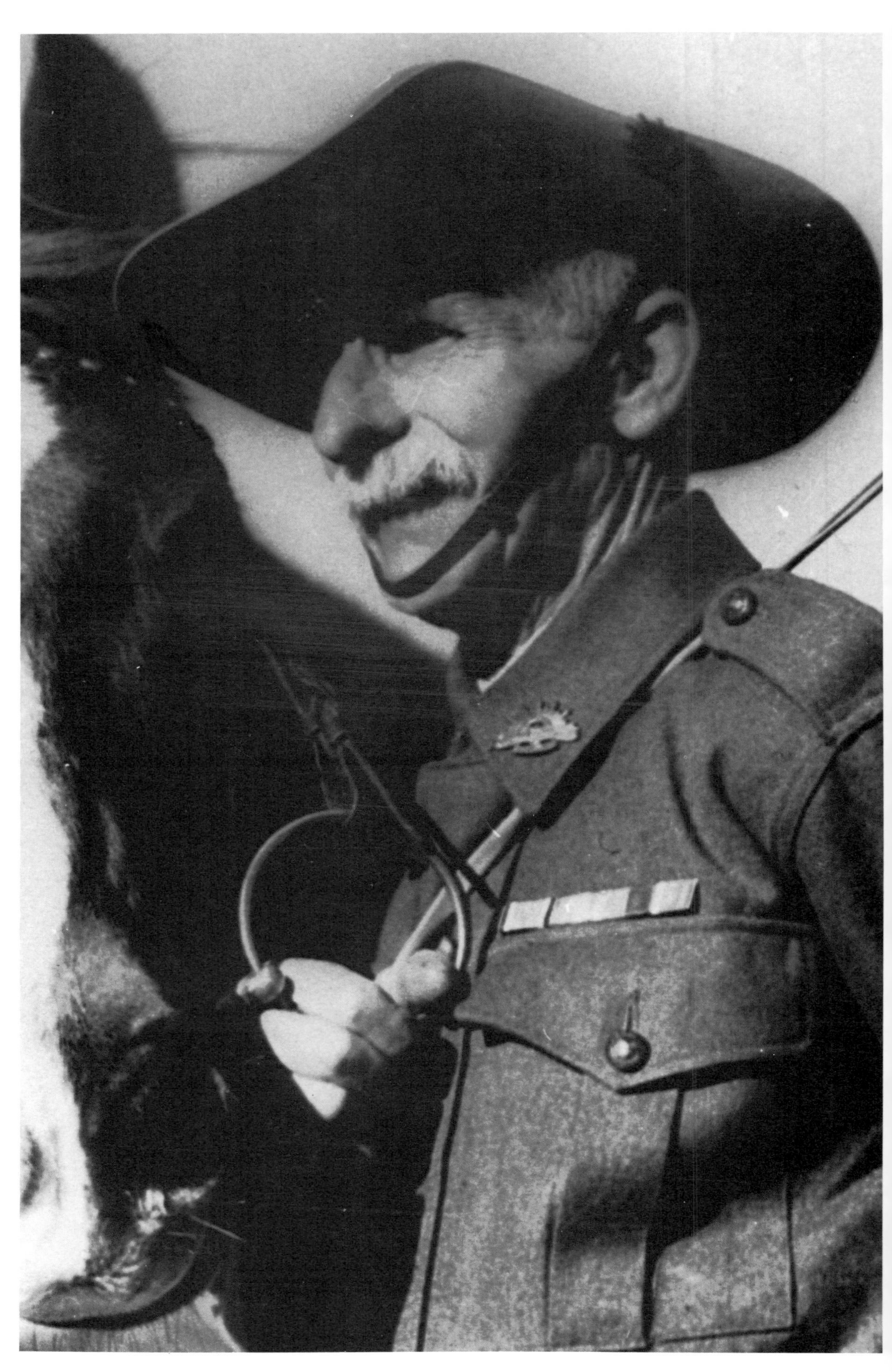

During 1942 beaches around Australia took on a Tobruk-like grimness as they were barricaded with barbed wire in an attempt to prevent an expected Japanese invasion. Many beaches were also mined. The public were barred from most beaches — a harsh measure for Australians — and unauthorised photographs of beach defences were not permitted to be taken. The installation of barbed wire was often undertaken by members of the Volunteer Defence Corps.

The playful looks of these children, the relaxed pose of the girl in the foreground and the exposed milk bottles cast some doubt on the seriousness or effectiveness of air-raid drills as they were practised in schools around Australia. The idea of air-raid precautions received considerable public support after the outbreak of war in 1939, but as the prospect that Australia would be a target for a German bombing attack seemed remote, interest soon waned. The Japanese threat, however, brought renewed interest, both popular and official, and a number of measures, many of them aimed at protecting schools and other institutional buildings, were introduced. Trenches were dug in school yards — although, as was pointed out, their usefulness in anything less than prolonged dry weather was questionable — many buildings were reinforced with sandbags, blackout measures were introduced and, in the large cities, air-raid sirens were installed to warn of impending attacks.

Air-raid drill became a feature of life in Australian cities and at the sound of a siren people took cover under beds or in often crudely designed 'shelters', like this one in a Melbourne kindergarten.

Trenches became the order of the day during 1942 — in school playgrounds, parks, and even in private backyards and gardens. In New South Wales the return to school after the Christmas holidays was delayed for two weeks to allow trenches, like those in the bottom right photograph, to be dug in school playgrounds. In some schools and public places more elaborate underground shelters, like the one in the Sydney Domain (*bottom left*), were constructed.

Individuals or groups of citizens sometimes attempted to build shelters of their own. The Adelaide children in the top picture are digging a trench, which they are covering with logs and sandbags.

On Sunday 31 May 1942 Sydney had its first of two direct experiences of war. Three Japanese midget submarines, each carrying two men and armed with two torpedoes, left a fleet of larger submarines standing off the coast, with the aim of sinking American and Australian ships in Sydney Harbour. Only two of the submarines got into the harbour. One became entangled in the protective netting that had been placed between the Heads; it was destroyed by its crew. One submarine fired its torpedoes at the United States cruiser *Chicago*; they missed and hit instead a former ferry, the *Kuttabul*, which had been converted into a floating naval barracks. The strike killed 19 men. The third submarine was destroyed by depth charges. It is seen (*top*) being retrieved from the harbour. The bottom photograph shows the half-submerged *Kuttabul* the morning after the incident.

As the attacks occurred in the dark, searchlights probed the harbour waters and guns roared in a vain attempt to locate and destroy the successful intruder.

The following Sunday, 7 June, Sydney was again under bombardment. This time five shells, fired from a Japanese submarine, struck the eastern suburbs of Bondi and Woollahra, damaging houses, flats and roadways and causing one broken arm — the only human casualty of the raid. This photograph of the damage caused to one house clearly shows the fatal potential of the attack. Newcastle, further to the north, was also shelled. These attacks intensified the alarm that had already been raised by a series of successful attacks on Australian mercantile and naval vessels off the east coast of Australia.

In July 1942 the Japanese landed at Buna and Gona on the northern coast of New Guinea and pushed southwards to occupy Kokoda, a village at the top of the Owen Stanley Range, where there was an airstrip. Their aim was to capture Port Moresby. They proceeded further south along the Kokoda Trail and came to within about 70 kilometres of their goal. On 23 September General Sir Thomas Blamey arrived in Port Moresby to take command of the Allied offensive that by the end of January 1943 would have driven the Japanese out of New Guinea. Here, General Blamey in Port Moresby inspects Australian troops that would soon be fighting on the Kokoda Trail.

Conditions on the Kokoda Trail were hazardous and difficult. Australian troops had to contend with extreme heat, tropical downpours, steep muddy terrain and raging torrents that had to be crossed. The photograph on the left shows the 'Golden Staircase', a particularly steep section consisting of 2000 steps cut into the side of the mountain. Malaria and other tropical diseases took a terrible toll, as did Japanese snipers who, cleverly camouflaged, abounded in the thick jungle. After the capture of Kokoda, in November, the fighting became easier. With the airstrip under Allied control, supplies could be brought in much more easily. On the right, a native of New Guinea — one of the 'Fuzzy Wuzzy Angels' — escorts a wounded Australian soldier to safety.

After the capture of Kokoda, Australian troops were airlifted to the north coast to clear the Japanese out of the area around Buna and Gona. Much of the savage and very close fighting took place in coconut plantations and swamps. Around Buna many Japanese had concealed themselves in bunkers beneath pieces of galvanised iron, like the one into which this Australian soldier is firing.

An occasional relief from the dangers and tensions of battle was provided by visiting groups of entertainers and musicians, whose activities and movements were coordinated from Pagewood in Sydney. Here, members of a swing band, the 'Tasmaniacs' — or, more properly, the Tasmanian Lines of Communication Concert Party — rehearse in a clearing on Bougainville Island before an evening performance for troops, in December 1944.

Despite some expressed misgivings about the long-term social consequences of allowing women to perform jobs that had hitherto been the preserve of men — a fear, for example, that women would develop a taste for paid work and a corresponding distaste for unpaid domestic work; or that money would corrupt women, who were unused to it — there was a ready acceptance during the war years of women conspicuously employed in a wide range of occupations. Women taxi-drivers and bread carters, for example, soon ceased being objects of amusement and comment. This woman is making home deliveries of bread in one of the horse-drawn and often colourfully designated bakers' vans that were common in the 1940s.

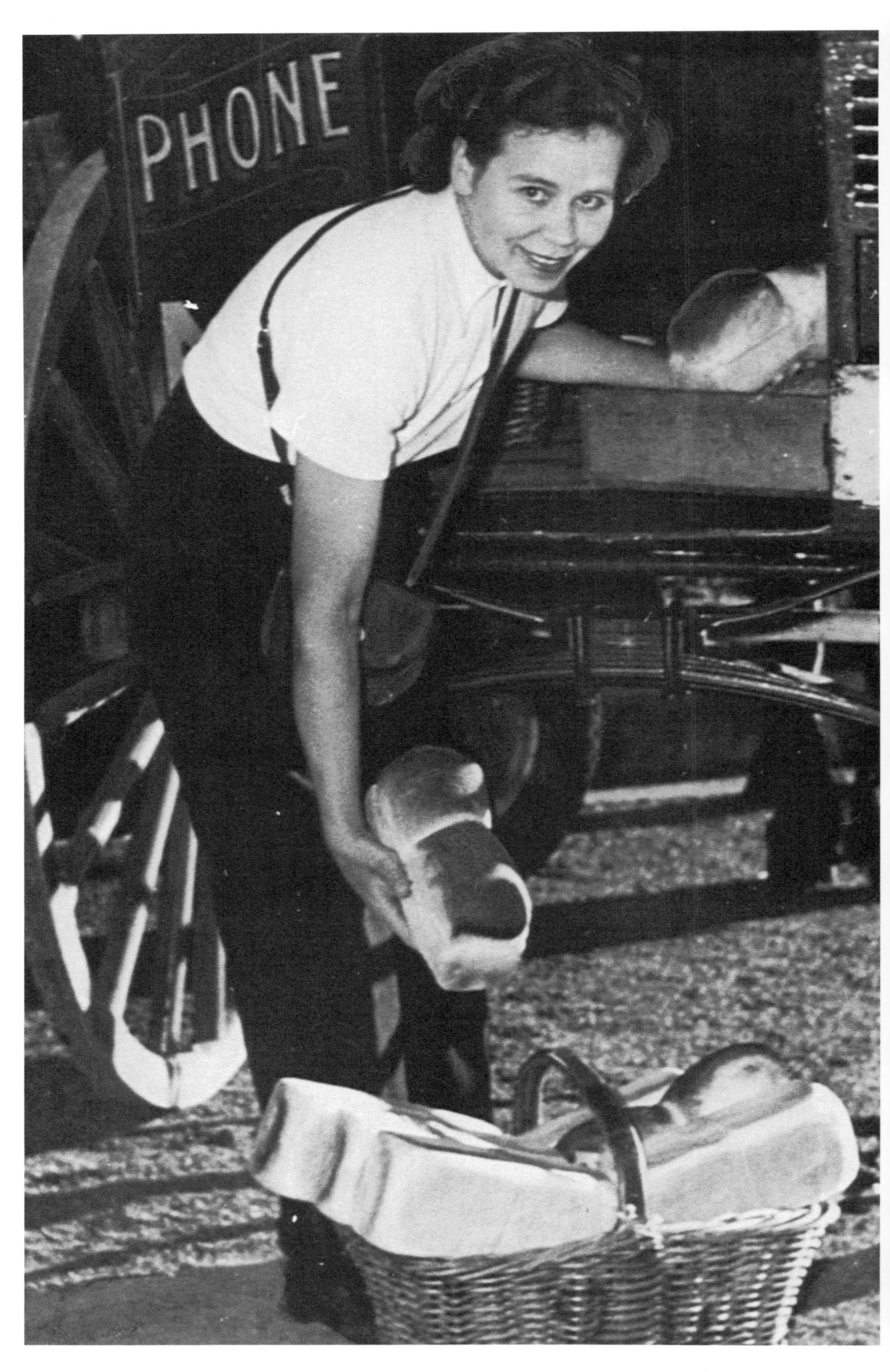

Women also made up for the shortage of male labour by working as 'posties' or in a variety of transport jobs. In February 1942, for example, there were more than 200 women employed by the Melbourne Tramways Board — many of them as conductresses — and recruitments of women numbered about 200 per week.

Munitions factories and other war-related manufacturing enterprises made extensive use of female labour. Many trade unionists opposed the entry of women into the workforce on the grounds that their lower wages — 50 to 60 per cent of male rates — made them a long-term threat to male employment. The ACTU demanded that women who replaced men be paid the same wage, and the issue was resolved by the formation of a Women's Employment Board, which set women's wages at no less than 60 per cent of the male wage for the same job. The three female workers in the photograph at bottom left were employed at the Commonwealth Air Corporation factory in Melbourne.

During the war the government assumed a considerable degree of control over citizens' lives. In 1942 Curtin won the approval of the government to send conscripted troops to fight in the immediate Pacific region. Men at home were also conscripted to work on essential projects and people in 'reserved' or essential jobs were required to remain in those jobs. Men between 45 and 60 could be called to serve in the Civil Constructional Corps and sent anywhere in the country to help build urgently needed roads, airports, factories and so on. These men, sometimes accompanied by their families, often had to endure Spartan conditions and primitive accommodation.

The invasion of Australian cities by American servicemen — both those on leave and those stationed here — provided a boost for the local entertainment and catering industries. Many businesses made available complimentary and reduced-price tickets to encourage the free-spending, often well-heeled, visitors to sample their wares. Here a group of Americans, in the specially set up 'Entertainment Bureau' in Sydney, survey the pickings for that evening.

The American visitors inspired ambivalent feelings in the Australian community. While businesses generally welcomed them and many young women took advantage of the social and sexual opportunities they offered, there was mutual resentment, fuelled by scenes like the one in the top photograph, that occasionally flared up into ugly incidents. The Australians were annoyed by the Americans' conspicuous affluence and their success with Australian girls; Americans often resented being conscripted to help defend Australia while many Australian troops remained at home. In an incident in Queensland that seems to epitomise the problems, a trainload of Australian soldiers heading north to embark and a trainload of Americans going southwards on leave became engaged in a violent and bloody battle.

American servicemen and their new-found Australian girlfriends, drinking the ubiquitous Coca-Cola, enjoy each other's company at an American Independence Day ball at the Melbourne Town Hall.

Petrol was in short supply during the whole of the war and for several years afterwards. Petrol rationing was introduced in 1940 and was made progressively more stringent as people either ignored the restrictions or devised ways of obtaining more than their entitlement of petrol. From 1942 citizens with no special allowances were entitled to only enough petrol to travel about 26 kilometres per week.

Some people got around the restrictions by fitting cumbersome devices known as 'gas-producers' to their cars. These ran on gases produced by the burning of charcoal but were extremely dirty and, because of the likelihood of an explosion, hazardous. Many, after trying these contraptions, became exasperated with them and made do with their petrol allowance and public transport. Two cars with gas-producers fitted are shown in the bottom photograph. One of the additions is discreetly concealed in the boot while the other is a disfiguring appendage on the back of the car.

The man in the top picture, eyeing the bags of charcoal on sale at this service station, seems to be considering the possibility of attaching a burner to his car. On this car its installation would have prevented the opening of the 'boot' to provide two open-air seats at the back.

Another, but equally cumbersome, way of beating the petrol shortage was to fill a balloon-like container with household gas and install it, as in this photograph, on a specially constructed rack on top of the vehicle.

One of the more elaborate examples of a 1940s petrol station, this one in the Sydney suburb of Concord has the rounded lines that typified much of the domestic and civic architecture, as well as the domestic furniture, of the period. The illuminated sign advertises 'Gas' instead of 'Petrol', an Americanism that can be attributed to the thousands of United States servicemen who visited or were stationed here.

The rationalisation of industry for the sake of the war effort and a drastic reduction in imports because of the dangers to shipping led to the rationing of food and other goods from June 1942. Tea, for example, was extremely short because the Japanese invasion of Java had cut off a major source of supply. Families were issued with coupons with which they could purchase specific quantities of particular goods. At first rationing procedures caused a good deal of confusion, and special counters, like this one in a Melbourne department store, were opened up to answer customers' rationing enquiries.

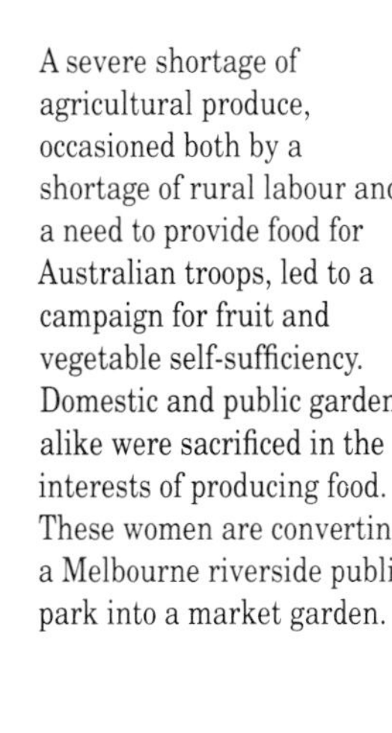

A severe shortage of agricultural produce, occasioned both by a shortage of rural labour and a need to provide food for Australian troops, led to a campaign for fruit and vegetable self-sufficiency. Domestic and public gardens alike were sacrificed in the interests of producing food. These women are converting a Melbourne riverside public park into a market garden.

Meat rationing did not begin until January 1944, but its introduction brought with it a bewildering complexity of regulations. Whereas other commodities were subject to simple quantity restrictions, the different cuts, types and qualities of meat meant that shoppers had to decipher charts like this one in order to determine what they were entitled to.

Two examples of wartime austerity: at left, boy scouts in Perth collect discarded rubber tyres for recycling; at right, kindergarten children in a Melbourne school construct a Christmas tree out of cut-up lengths of scrap paper and a piece of waste timber.

From 1941 Italian, German and Japanese prisoners of war arrived in Australia and were accommodated in camps that were set up in all states except Queensland. In all, about 25 000 prisoners of war came to Australia during World War II; the vast majority of them — more than 18 000 — were Italians. The Italians, in particular, made a significant contribution to overcoming Australia's manpower shortage, and in 1943 almost 14 000 of them were transferred from camps in India specifically to work in rural areas. The top picture shows a work party, comprising prisoners of all three nationalities, being returned to the camp at Murchison in Victoria at the end of a day.

In general the camps ran smoothly. One notable exception occurred on 5 August 1944 at the camp at Cowra in New South Wales. Just over 1100 Japanese prisoners, armed with baseball bats, sharpened garden tools and other improvised weapons, charged the barbed wire fences around the camp in a suicidal attempt to break out. In the episode 232 prisoners and four guards died. Of the 334 prisoners who escaped, 25 were killed and the rest were recaptured within nine days. The Japanese soldier (*bottom*), being repatriated at the end of the war, carries the ashes of a comrade killed in the Cowra breakout.

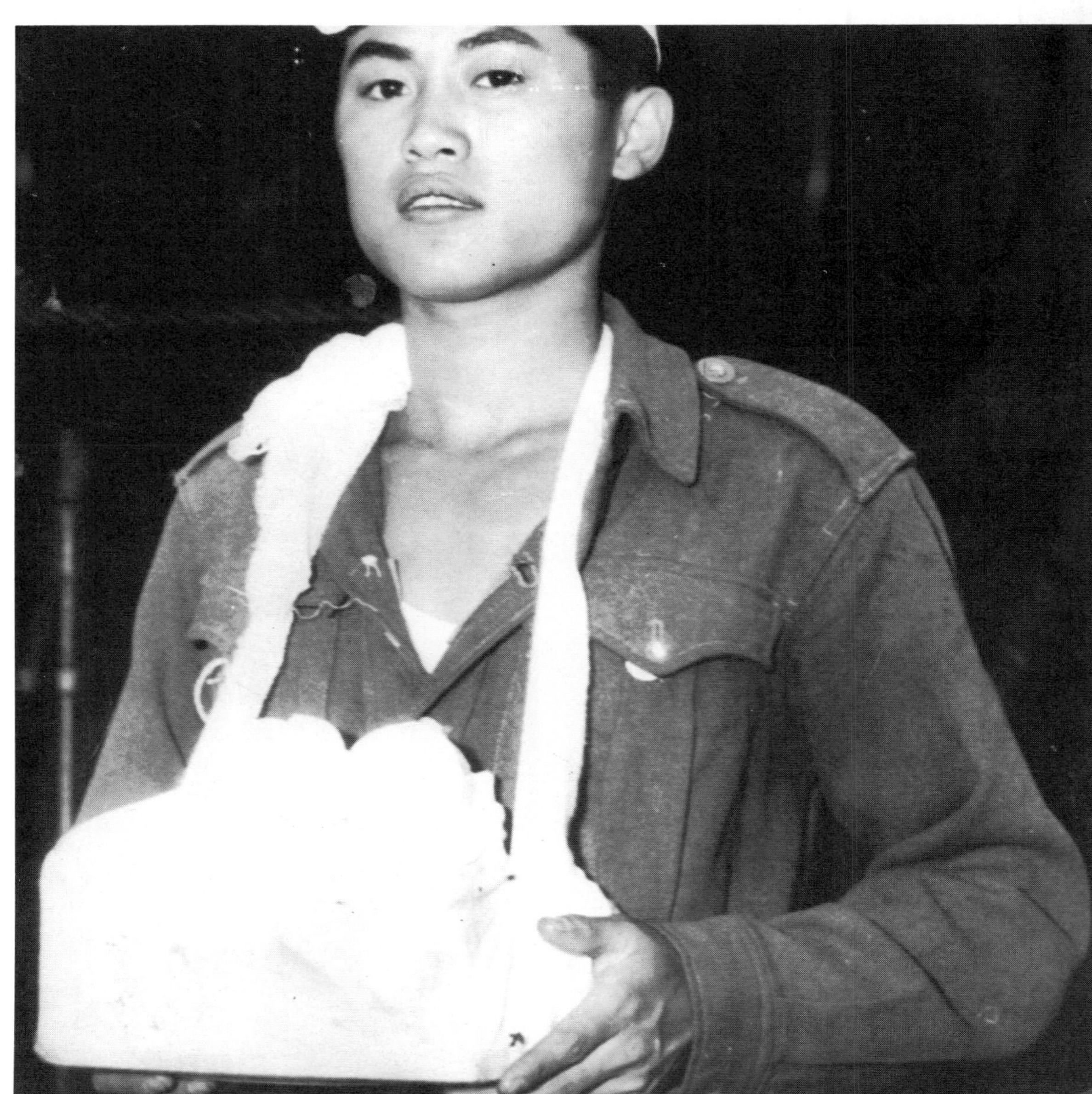

The internment of 'enemy aliens' began the day after war was declared. The percentage of aliens arrested was lower than during World War I, however, and the general community attitude was less extreme. Nineteen Japanese living in Victoria were interned at one of the camps at Tatura, mainly for their own protection. When they were joined by members of their families from other parts of Australia their numbers swelled to a thousand. They were more fortunate than many other internees in that they could live as a community and maintain their cultural and social traditions. Weddings, births — and about a hundred deaths — were all part of the Japanese experience at Tatura. This photograph shows a wedding group at the camp.

Over 22 000 Australians became prisoners of the Japanese during the war and almost 8000 of these died during their captivity. Most were captured when Singapore fell in February 1942. They were kept in the infamous Changi camp in Singapore, where they suffered numerous privations, including a wholly inadequate diet. Throughout the war prisoners from Changi were taken to various parts of Japanese-occupied Asia to work, often under appalling conditions, on the construction of railways, roads and airfields. During the building of the Burma railway almost 3000 Australians perished. This photograph shows emaciated Australian prisoners in Changi just after they had been liberated.

The last Australian military campaigns of the war were in Borneo and were commanded by Lieutenant-General Sir Leslie Morshead. Between 1 May and July 1945 Australian troops made a number of landings on both the north-east and west coasts of Borneo and by 22 July had secured the area. This photograph shows soldiers from the 7th Division landing, from an American ship, at the oil port of Balikpapan on the south-east coast on 1 July.

Japanese surrender was forced by the dropping of atomic bombs, by the Americans, on the Japanese cities of Hiroshima and Nagasaki in August 1945. While General Macarthur accepted the general surrender on 2 September, various Australian commanders accepted the surrenders of Japanese commanders in the eastern part of the Dutch East Indies, Borneo and in the Australian Territories. Here Lieutenant-General S. G. Savige accepts the Japanese surrender on Bougainville Island.

At 9.30 on the morning of Wednesday 15 August 1945, Prime Minister Chifley began an address to the nation with the words, 'Fellow citizens, the war is over'. It was a signal for universal rejoicing. In the cities people poured out of offices onto the streets in a spontaneous expression of happy relief. In Sydney crowds estimated at about a million thronged the streets, singing, dancing and shouting their joy. The spirit of the occasion is captured in this photograph in which a sailor in uniform flourishes a newspaper poster proclaiming 'Peace', and two young women exuberantly sport the caps of the sailors who have lifted them onto their shoulders.

On the next day, 16 August, victory parades were held. Here, in Sydney, a pipe band leads a procession of civilians and service personnel along Macquarie Street. Despite the official nature of the occasion a certain irreverent wit still crept into the proceedings: one of the signs held aloft designates its followers as 'Ancillary Corps Tramps 1939-45'.

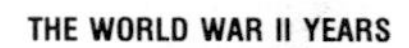

In November 1946 the first post-war federal election was held. The opposition was led by Robert Gordon Menzies who, although he resigned from the leadership of the United Australia Party in 1941, had regained it after the big Labor win in 1943. In October 1944 a conference of anti-Labor organisations produced a new party, the Liberal party, with Menzies at its head. At the 1946 elections Menzies campaigned on a platform of reduced personal taxation and tough measures against illegal strikes, while the Labor government under Chifley, with its wartime record behind it, advocated full employment, increased welfare benefits and tight economic controls. Labor won with a comfortable majority. Here Menzies faces a noisy election rally, confronted by signs and shouts of 'Pig-Iron Bob', in unforgiving memory of his determination to sell scrap iron to Japan in 1939.

John Curtin died in office on 5 July 1945. A week later, his Treasurer and close friend, Joseph Benedict ('Ben') Chifley, was elected leader of the Labor Party and so became Prime Minister. Although Chifley, pictured here in the House of Representatives, lacked flamboyance he was able to dominate the parliament with his calm and deliberate manner.

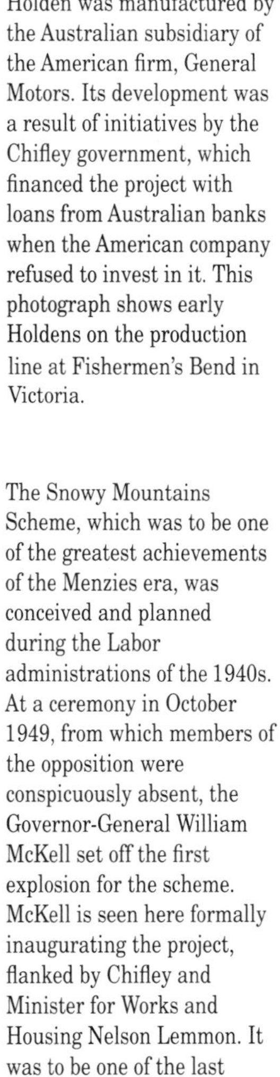

The Holden car, which dominated Australian roads throughout the 1950s, was still a novelty at the end of the 1940s. The first model came off the production line on 29 November 1948. Production increased steadily, until by 1962 the millionth Holden had been made. Promoted and generally accepted as 'Australia's own car', the Holden was manufactured by the Australian subsidiary of the American firm, General Motors. Its development was a result of initiatives by the Chifley government, which financed the project with loans from Australian banks when the American company refused to invest in it. This photograph shows early Holdens on the production line at Fishermen's Bend in Victoria.

The Snowy Mountains Scheme, which was to be one of the greatest achievements of the Menzies era, was conceived and planned during the Labor administrations of the 1940s. At a ceremony in October 1949, from which members of the opposition were conspicuously absent, the Governor-General William McKell set off the first explosion for the scheme. McKell is seen here formally inaugurating the project, flanked by Chifley and Minister for Works and Housing Nelson Lemmon. It was to be one of the last ceremonies at which Chifley would officiate as Prime Minister; within two months his government would be defeated and Menzies would once again be Prime Minister.

In March 1945 Chifley, as Treasurer, introduced two Banking Acts that established significant government control over the private trading banks, and allowed the government to control the supply of money. In 1947, when part of this legislation was declared unconstitutional, Chifley decided to nationalise the trading banks. The decision was responsible, more than anything else, for Labor's defeat at the 1949 election. A wave of protest was orchestrated by the banks and the opposition, who claimed that the move was tantamount to 'communising' Australia. Some demonstrations in favour of nationalisation were held, like the one shown here, but most Australians responded to the alarms raised by its opponents.

Another event that provided ammunition for the government's opponents was a nation-wide coal strike, which lasted for seven weeks during the winter of 1949. The strike, organised by communists, was for higher wages, shorter working hours and long-service leave. The strike eventually ended when troops were brought in to operate the mines. Although the government took strong measures against the strikers, the opposition was able to capitalise on an alleged connection between communism and Labor. These striking miners carry placards stating their demands and expressing the perennial grievances about the double standards of self-serving politicians.

The Liberal and Country parties won a very easy victory at the elections held on 10 December 1949, and Robert Gordon Menzies, seen here confidently campaigning on a dais draped with the British flag, became Prime Minister for the second time. Few at the time could have guessed that he would prove such a powerful and enduring political force. He was to remain Prime Minister for an uninterrupted sixteen years, until his retirement in 1966, and Labor was to be denied office for another twenty-three years.

7
The Menzies Era
1949 – 1970

In the sixteen years during which he presided over the government of Australia, Menzies gave an impression of invulnerability, and the conservative forces of the Liberal and Country parties promoted themselves as the 'natural' government of the country. Menzies established an absolute dominance over the Liberal Party and led it, in coalition with the Country Party, to victory in seven successive elections. He did, however, come very close to defeat in 1961 and was maintained in power only by preferences from the Democratic Labor Party, a strongly anti-communist organisation that consisted mainly of defectors from the Labor Party during its great split of 1955. Menzies' urbanity, his lightning and often scathing wit and his ardent pro-Britishness appealed to an increasingly affluent electorate, who were reaping the material benefits of the industrial post-war expansion and the high prices that Australia's wheat and other agricultural products — and later its mineral resources — could command overseas.

The 1950s and 1960s were Australia's 'lucky country' era. Despite the tensions of the Cold War, Australians generally enjoyed a period of unprecedented material wealth. The confidence that good times were here to stay was reflected in the rapid expansion of personal debt, as people bought all manner of consumer goods on hire purchase and took out large loans from banks and other financial institutions to buy their own homes.

Menzies and his governments were staunchly anti-communist and were able to capitalise on fears of domestic communist infiltration in order to win votes, and to use the threat of communist expansion in South-East Asia as a justification for involvement in Asian wars. Between 1940 and 1958 almost 2000 Australians were killed in the inconclusive Korean War and from 1965 Australian volunteers, and then conscripts, were sent to fight in Vietnam. The Australian involvement in Vietnam at first had widespread community approval, which was gradually whittled away, however, as internal opposition became more vociferous and as the futility of the exercise became more apparent.

Much of the opposition to the war in Vietnam came from the educated young, who during the 1960s assertively rejected many prevailing community standards. Student militancy increased greatly during the period and found in the Vietnam War, as well in a number of other issues, a cause with which it could identify. Along with this, and helped by the availability of the contraceptive pill, went a new-found freedom from sexual restraint that caused the sixties to be dubbed 'the permissive age'.

Previous pages: In 1965, only months before his retirement as Prime Minister, Sir Robert Menzies was appointed Lord Warden of the Cinque Ports and Constable of Dover Castle. It was a fitting final honour for an Australian who had shown such unswerving loyalty to Britain and the monarchy.

Left: During the sixties young people in Australia, like those in other Western countries, rejected many of the constraints that had previously been placed on them. A new 'permissiveness', reflected in greater sexual freedom as well as in more active involvement in political and social issues, became the norm. This picture suggests something of the spirit of the times.

In the migrant intake that began soon after the end of World War II and continued through to the 1970s people of British origin formed by far the largest ethnic group. Shiploads of assisted British migrants arrived in Australia's capital cities, many of them sponsored by friends and relatives. Most, like the large family in the top photograph, were buoyed up by the prospect of new experiences and fresh, but as yet unknown, opportunities. Others, like the new arrivals (*bottom*) disembarking in Melbourne from the *Ranchi* in August 1950, had a clearer idea of what lay in store. They had been brought to Australia by the Victorian Railways and had both houses and jobs to go to.

Australia's mass intake of continental European migrants began at the end of 1947 when almost 1000 displaced persons from the Baltic countries landed in Melbourne under an assisted migration scheme sponsored by the federal government. Reaction to their entry, and that of subsequent arrivals, was generally favourable, despite a few rumblings from organisations and individuals who were alarmed about the introduction of 'alien elements'. Between 1947 and 1954 a quarter of a million displaced persons from Europe were resettled in Australia. In this photograph a group of Baltic migrants take a much-appreciated meal at the refreshment rooms of Victoria's Seymour Station on their way to the Bonegilla migrant camp.

Migrant camps, like this one at Villawood in Sydney, were built during the 1950s in the suburbs of capital cities to provide accommodation for migrants who had nowhere else to go. Many migrants were so disillusioned by the physical discomfort, lack of hygiene and the regimented nature of hostel life that they returned home very soon after arriving.

By 1966, when this photograph was taken, distinctive Italian and Greek faces were no longer a novelty in Australia, and much of the prejudice against foreigners, and especially against the sound of strange languages, had been broken down. Many younger migrants established themselves in Australia before bringing out their parents and setting up the extended family groups that still characterise migrant communities. Here, the young Greek woman and her child are on the deck of the *Patris*, ready to disembark in Melbourne.

One of the most commonly expounded justifications for Australia's post-war immigration policies was the need for labour to expand Australian industries. Migrants, it was claimed, would both contribute to and reap the benefits of Australia's prosperity. As a general rule, however, migrants were employed in unskilled and often poorly paid jobs. A survey undertaken in Melbourne in 1966 found that more than a third of Italian and close to a half of Greek migrants were employed in what were classified as unskilled manual jobs. This group of Italians, photographed in 1952 working for the Victorian Railways, had very little prospect of ever finding more congenial employment.

One of the greatest sources of employment for migrants of all nationalities was the Snowy Mountains Scheme, the most ambitious engineering project ever undertaken by an Australian government. Without the migrants, who comprised by far the greatest part of the workforce, this vast series of dams and tunnels, which would be the source of much of the country's electricity and would supply irrigation to areas of western New South Wales, could not have been built. For some aspects of the scheme specialist skills that were not available in Australia were needed. Norwegian specialists were brought in, for example, to advise and help in the construction of huge tunnels, like the one shown here that would take water from Lake Eucumbene to Tumut.

Repetitive and poorly paid jobs in the textile industry were all that were available to many young migrant women who lacked both qualifications and a working knowledge of English.

Post-war immigration brought with it many cultural influences that helped to change aspects of Australian tastes and lifestyles. In sport, for example, soccer gained enormously in popularity, both as a spectator and a participatory sport. New soccer clubs, with names like Slavia and Hellas (seen here in a match in 1964), were at first the preserve of their migrant founders, but later achieved much wider membership and following.

In the 1950s particularly, tennis was one of Australia's great boom sports. Hordes of middle-class youngsters spent the greater part of their weekends and school holidays on tennis courts, inspired by the feats of players like Lew Hoad (left) and Ken Rosewall (extreme right), seen here with the other victorious members of the 1955 Davis Cup team. Harry Hopman (centre), the man credited by most as the force responsible for the great revival of Australian tennis, was the non-playing captain of the team.

In November and December 1956, the sixteenth modern Olympic Games were held in Melbourne. Hundreds of thousands of visitors poured into the city and over 100 000 watched the spectacular opening ceremony at the Melbourne Cricket Ground on 22 November. Aspro devised a peculiarly Australian welcome for the visitors, whose headaches and hangovers it no doubt hoped could be assuaged by its product. The promoters, however, probably did not foresee that their elevated advertisement would be the subject of wry amusement and ribald comment.

Two of Australia's greatest swimming stars, Lorraine Crapp and Dawn Fraser (*left*), represented Australia at the Melbourne Olympics, and between them won three gold medals. Australia's total of 13 gold medals represented a significant improvement over its previous record of six, established in 1952. By general consent, however, the hero of the Melbourne Olympics was the Russian runner Vladimir Kuts, who won the 5000 and 10 000 metre events. Kuts impressed, not only by his athletic brilliance, but by sportingly allowing an Australian runner to beat him in a heat of the 5000 metre run. He is seen here (*right*) crossing the finishing line, a clear winner in the final.

The one ugly incident that occurred during the Melbourne Olympics had its origins in events in Europe. Russian tanks had recently rolled into Hungary and put down the popular uprising there. Hungarian athletes had come to Melbourne in small groups and often under great difficulties. They had been supplied with such basic equipment as running shoes and swimming trunks by members of the British team. During a water polo match between the Hungarian and Russian teams a scuffle broke out in the water and the Hungarian Ervin Zador emerged from the pool with a cut eye. He is pictured here being spoken to by the referee, as spectators, still confused about what has happened, rise to their feet. Just after this, booing broke out in the crowd and police had to be called to restore order and prevent further violence.

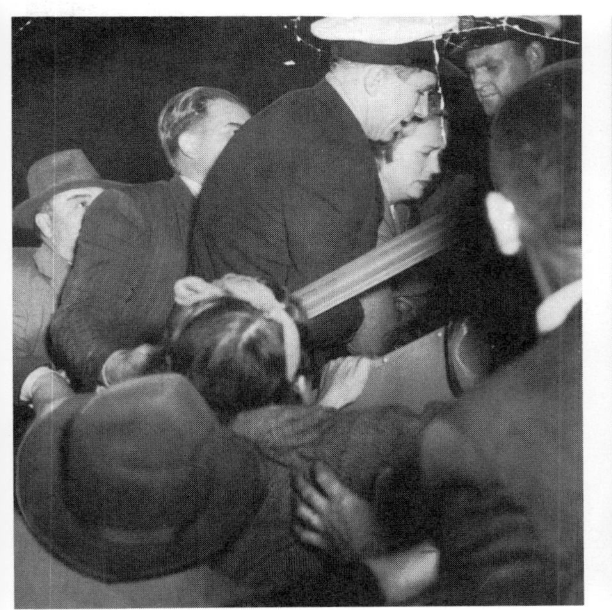

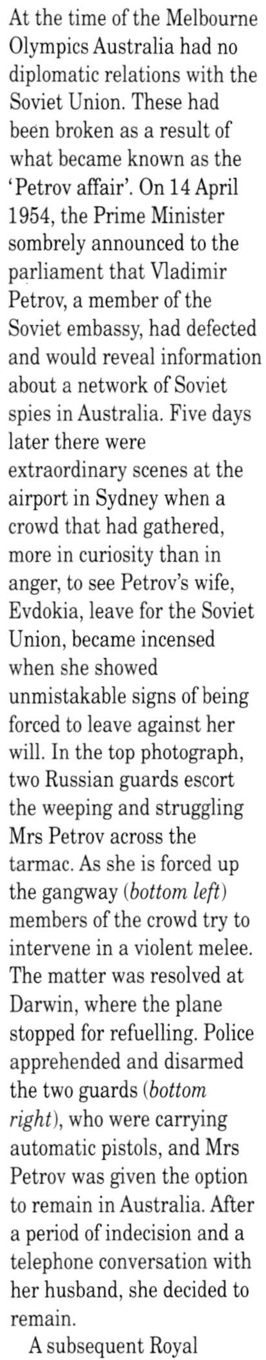

At the time of the Melbourne Olympics Australia had no diplomatic relations with the Soviet Union. These had been broken as a result of what became known as the 'Petrov affair'. On 14 April 1954, the Prime Minister sombrely announced to the parliament that Vladimir Petrov, a member of the Soviet embassy, had defected and would reveal information about a network of Soviet spies in Australia. Five days later there were extraordinary scenes at the airport in Sydney when a crowd that had gathered, more in curiosity than in anger, to see Petrov's wife, Evdokia, leave for the Soviet Union, became incensed when she showed unmistakable signs of being forced to leave against her will. In the top photograph, two Russian guards escort the weeping and struggling Mrs Petrov across the tarmac. As she is forced up the gangway (*bottom left*) members of the crowd try to intervene in a violent melee. The matter was resolved at Darwin, where the plane stopped for refuelling. Police apprehended and disarmed the two guards (*bottom right*), who were carrying automatic pistols, and Mrs Petrov was given the option to remain in Australia. After a period of indecision and a telephone conversation with her husband, she decided to remain.

A subsequent Royal Commission, which did not result in any prosecutions being brought, confirmed many people in the belief that the whole episode had been exploited by the Prime Minister for political gain.

Menzies' announcement of Petrov's defection and its possible dire implications was all the more dramatic because it was made to a nation still enjoying the euphoric afterglow of the first visit to these shores by a reigning British monarch. The young, beautiful, and universally admired Queen Elizabeth II (who had been on her way to Australia two years earlier when her father died) and her handsome consort, Prince Philip, had left Australia only twelve days earlier, after an exhausting two-month tour. Wherever they went they had been besieged by adoring crowds, and newspapers and popular magazines had vied with each other in their desire to give the fullest possible coverage of the tour.

In the top picture, lines of soldiers act as barricades as a huge Sydney crowd greets the royal motorcade. The bottom picture shows the royal couple waving to well-wishers from the back of the specially appointed train. Such matters as the lavish details of the train's appointments and the minutiae of the Queen's wardrobe and coiffure were extensively covered in the media and lapped up by a curious and grateful populace.

While it is probable that Menzies gained a lot of political kudos from the royal visit and from being seen and photographed so often with the monarch — and that this was reflected in the elections that took place only weeks later — there can be no doubt of his devotion to and real affection for the young Queen. As they arrive together for an official function Her Majesty, hurriedly adjusting one of her gloves, seems to be steeling herself for an ordeal; the Prime Minister positively beams with pride and pleasure.

Television, the exciting new medium that within a decade was to transform Australian domestic life and entertainment patterns, came to Sydney and Melbourne in September 1956, just in time for the Olympic Games. The first transmission, on 16 September, was on TCN Channel 9 in Sydney and featured, among some nervous studio presentation and imported American comedy programs, Australia's first TV commercial — for Rothman's cigarettes. Less than a year later Melbourne and Sydney had three channels each — one ABC and two commercial — which screened a total of about 120 hours a week. By 1960 all Australian capitals had regular television programs. Although the standard fare consisted of imported — and especially American — programs, a number of local programs were made and Australian television stars emerged. None proved more durable than the young Melbourne entertainer Graham Kennedy, seen here in 1958, who for fourteen years from 1957 compèred the popular variety show 'In Melbourne Tonight'.

The official commencement of television transmission in Melbourne — by GTV 9 — was marked by the carefully stage-managed arrival in the studio of the Governor of Victoria Sir Dallas Brookes, in a black limousine. The hand-picked and sartorially splendid audience applaud his entrance while a group of notables wait to greet him and to be among the first Australians to grace the small silver screen.

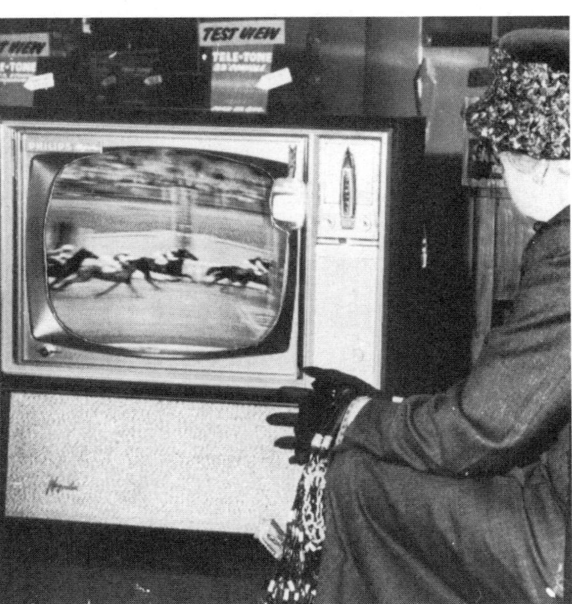

In the affluent fifties, teenagers were targeted by advertisers as consumers in their own right. Television, too, catered for their tastes with shows like 'Six O'Clock Rock' and 'Bandstand'. This session of 'Six O'Clock Rock' (*left*), starring the rock star Johnny O'Keefe, is being relayed from the ABC's Sydney studios.

Television offered enormous scope for the transmission of sporting events. In 1960 the Melbourne Cup was televised for the first time (*right*).

The teenage culture that was a feature of the 1950s and 1960s was never more evident than during the visit in 1964 of the British rock group, the Beatles. Their visit received saturation media coverage and wherever they appeared they were able to rouse their fans, especially the female ones, into a state of hysterical frenzy. In this photograph the four entertainers appear on a balcony after their arrival at Melbourne airport, as a large contingent of police struggle to keep a cheering, waving and jostling crowd under control.

The arrival of the Beatles in Sydney was marked by scenes like this one in which police link hands in a determined and desperate effort to protect the group from their equally determined and seemingly possessed admirers.

The much-vaunted permissiveness, as well as the idealism, of the youth of the sixties found perhaps its most potent theatrical expression in the American rock musical *Hair*, which came to Australia in 1969. *Hair* achieved enormous notoriety because of its unashamed use of taboo words and because in one scene its entire cast stood facing the audience entirely naked — although voyeurs had their expectations largely foiled by the subtle lighting. The message of *Hair*, well attuned to the times, was one of unbridled love and idyllic peace. At the end of the show audience and cast danced and sang on stage. Here Graham Kennedy gets into the act after the opening performance in Sydney.

The mini-skirt came, rather belatedly, to Australia when the English model Jean Shrimpton, nicknamed 'The Shrimp', defied some hallowed racing traditions and wore this simple but effective outfit to Melbourne's Flemington Racecourse on Derby Day, the Saturday before Cup Day, in 1965. While the hatted, gloved and stockinged women in the background regarded her with looks ranging from indifference to outright mirth, Shrimpton struck a flamboyant pose that next day was seen in newspapers all over the country.

By the end of the decade people would have wondered how such an inoffensive dress as the one worn by Shrimpton could have caused such a furore. A skirt that exposed a mere 10 centimetres of thigh would have looked decidedly demure on a young lady of 1969 or 1970. By that time the smart young woman was likely to be seen in public dressed something like this — but preferably in more salubrious surroundings.

Not only were hemlines going up in the early sixties; ever more uncovered midriffs were appearing on the nation's beaches and, according to some, taking an ever-increasing toll on the nation's moral fibre. The bikini was a product of the late 1940s but gained prominence in Australia when the designer Paula Stafford introduced it to Gold Coast beaches. This photograph shows the original and startlingly brief Stafford bikinis.

Photographs like the one on the left, designed to titillate susceptible males, adorned many an evening tabloid during the late fifties and early sixties.

Some beach inspectors, as arbiters of public decency, adopted a strictly legalistic approach to the bikini problem. The woman *(right)*, on Bondi Beach in 1961, is trying to prove to the inspectors that her bikini covers the requisite 3 inches (7.5 centimetres) at the sides.

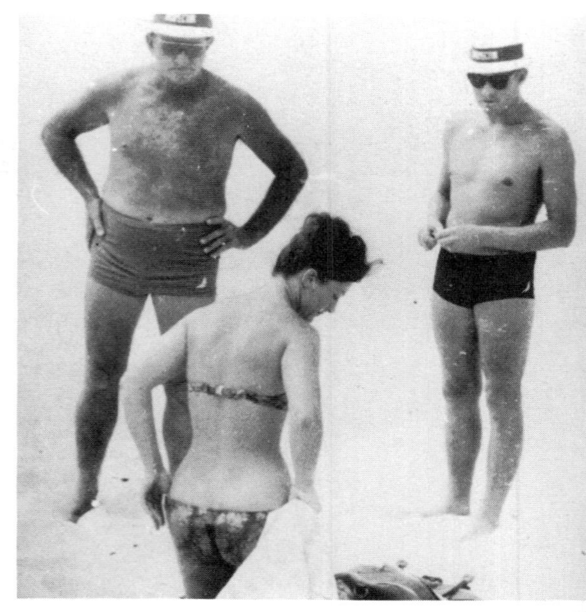

Menzies' successor as Prime Minister was Harold Holt. His personal style, if not his political persuasions, were very different from those of his august predecessor. He posed for this photograph, with his step-daughters-in-law, at Portsea near Melbourne just after assuming the Prime Ministership in January 1966. He was well aware that the photo would be widely published and commented upon, and that the ladies' relatively abbreviated swimsuits would help promote his image as a leader in touch with the latest trends. It was not far from here that Holt disappeared while swimming, less than two years later.

Holt's brief period as Prime Minister was marked by bitter debate, and often violent demonstrations, about the government's staunch support for the American war effort in Vietnam. During 1966 the United States increased its troop numbers in Vietnam eightfold and brought pressure on Australia for increased support. In March 1966, just eleven months after the first Australian combat troops had been committed, the first conscripted Australian servicemen were sent to serve in the war; two months later the first conscript had been killed. Soon after, Holt visited the United States and virtually locked Australia into further commitment when he coined his famous catchcry, 'All the way with LBJ'. In October 1966 US President Lyndon Baines Johnson himself came all the way to Australia to express his gratitude for Australia's support and to ensure that the support continued. His visit was remarkable for the massive welcome he received from crowds around the country and also for the angry demonstrations that were staged by the minority, consisting mainly of the young, who at this stage opposed the war and Australian involvement in it. In this demonstration in Sydney demonstrators bearing a forest of placards try to break through a police cordon to reach the presidential motorcade.

In November 1966 an election was fought mainly on the issue of Vietnam. Holt's government was returned with a greatly increased majority.

Australian soldiers in the jungles of South Vietnam investigate a hut that may be concealing Vietcong guerillas.

Throughout the late 1960s many young Australian men who opposed the government's Vietnam policy either refused to register for national service or failed to report when called up. This conscientious objector is unceremoniously arrested at his Sydney home by three extremely burly uniformed police and one plain clothes man, while his friends and supporters demonstrate in opposition to the war.

On 5 October 1966 there were nationwide marches and demonstrations against conscription. In an attempt to curb demonstrations generally and public opposition to the Vietnam war particularly, the Queensland government had used the provisions of the Traffic Act to restrict people's right to participate in street marches. Twenty-six of these students from the University of Queensland were arrested for taking part in this protest. No arrests were made anywhere else in Australia.

Although Vietnam was the focus of the protests, many of the posters carried in this and in other demonstrations indicated an opposition to war in general and reflected the strong pacifist tendencies that existed among students in the sixties.

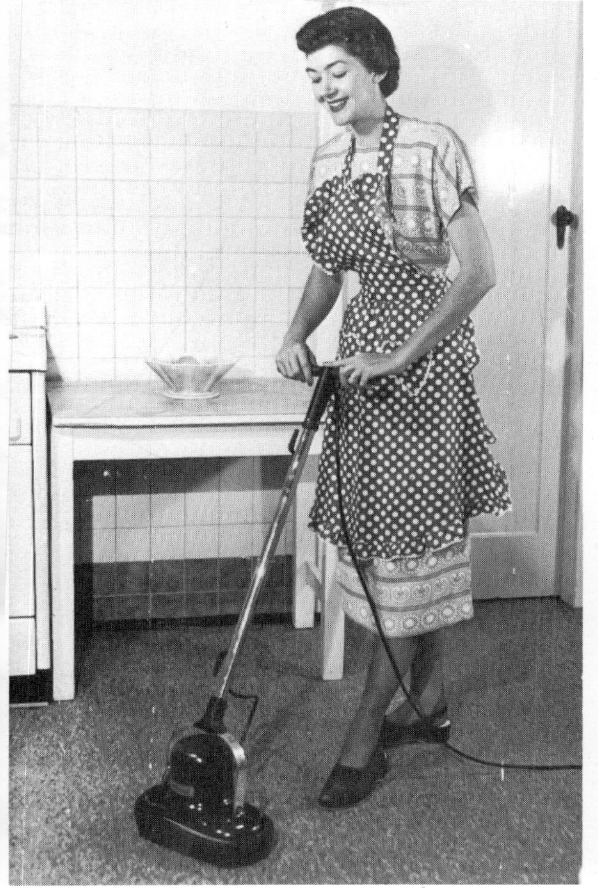

Stirrings of female militancy that would blossom into the full-blown and aggressive 'women's liberation' movement of the seventies, became progressively more insistent during the sixties. While cries for 'liberation' were sometimes heard and gestures like the public burning of bras attracted often condescending media attention, the main thrust of the movement at this stage was for women to be paid the same amount as men for the same or equivalent work. 'Equal pay for equal work' was the ideal striven and, frequently, demonstrated for. The top picture shows barmaids, striking for equal pay, carrying their placards through the streets of Newcastle in New South Wales in 1962.

In 1969 the Arbitration Court, in a ruling that contained a number of ambiguities and that stipulated a three-year phasing-in period, accepted the principle of equal pay for women.

The idea that 'a woman's place is in the home' still held sway among more conservative elements during the 1960s and received ample reinforcement in advertising of domestic products on television and in other media. Ironically, far from tying women more securely to their homes, the easier availability of time-saving appliances like the ones shown in the bottom two photographs, helped to make outside employment possible for many married women.

These interiors were fairly typical of the environments in which many lower-middle to working-class families lived, and in which women worked, during the 1950s. Except for the patterned linoleum floor and the vases of flowers — probably placed there for the photograph — the kitchen has been designed along functional rather than aesthetic lines. The canisters on the mantelpiece would have contained those items — tea, sugar, flour and so on — that were regularly used, and there is a small airing cupboard with a wire-screen door for commodities that might become musty in a closed space. The fuel stove was used for range-top cooking, and for heating the room in winter, and there is an electric oven on the left. Hot water is not laid on, although there would probably have been a gas or electric water heater over the bathtub. By this time a refrigerator, on the right hand side here, was standard in all but the poorest homes. The family would have taken their meals around the small wooden table; the lighter laminex and chrome tables and vinyl-covered chairs became popular in the sixties.

The lounge room, on the other hand, is almost oppressively plush with its bulky velvet-covered lounge suite, its richly patterned carpet and thick, heavy drapes that would have excluded any daylight. Except for the new electric heater with its imitation glowing coals the room harks back to the forties rather than looks forward to the sixties, by which time leaner, lighter-looking furniture had come into vogue.

This New South Wales Housing Commission house was one of a number built in the Sydney suburb of Concord in the 1950s and, except that it is constructed of brick, is typical of many of the more modest dwellings of that era. Built on a small block with a neat but perfunctory garden, the house, like those of previous decades but unlike the ones that were to follow, seems to have been built to keep the daylight out and makes no provision for covered outdoor living.

Soaring blocks of flats, like these ones built by the Victorian Housing Commission on reclaimed land at Williamstown, were designed as part of a plan to provide alternative forms of high-density housing. In many ways they were worse than what they replaced, denying most of their occupants easy access to the outside and creating an alienating and depressing sense of anonymity. Their rigid functionalism and stylistic barrenness made them conspicuous blots on the cityscape. Similar blocks were also built in parts of Sydney and, to a lesser extent, in other capital cities.

Four city scenes during the 1960s:
Top left: The richly ornamented Victorian facades of buildings in Melbourne's beautiful Collins Street during the 1950s. The progressive destruction of many of these buildings over the next twenty years to make way for the inexorable thrust skywards was the subject of a great deal of bitter controversy and anguished protest.
Top right: A construction worker descends from the upper levels of a rising new building into the sunless chasms that much of Sydney's high-rise development has created.
Bottom left: This multi-storeyed carpark with its hundreds of jutting balconies was symptomatic of the strains the motor car was imposing on conditions in Sydney's central business district.
Bottom right: Like a giant filing cabinet, the Sydney Water Board building, photographed from in front of the Town Hall, dwarfs an adjacent, more humanly proportioned, Victorian building.

In marked contrast to most other Sydney buildings of the period, Harry Seidler's arresting white circular Australia Square Tower, built in 1967, is an example of imaginative high-rise design.

The relentless spread of suburbia and the almost universal ownership of and reliance on the motor car gave rise to the development during the 1960s of sometimes vast regional shopping centres that aimed to cater for the entire shopping needs of their immediate and surrounding communities, and to remove the necessity for people to travel into the centres of the capital cities. Competition between these centres was often keen, and managements resorted to such gimmickry as live entertainment, give-away prizes, and sometimes outlandishly decorated and festooned interior spaces to lure people to particular complexes. This one is the Chadstone shopping centre in suburban Melbourne.

The Sidney Myer Music Bowl, built in 1959 in the King's Domain, Melbourne, and named after the city's most famous retailing pioneer, was, with its imaginative evocation of a vast tent, a welcome addition to Melbourne's architectural scene and to its cultural life. It inspired a number of similar, but much less imposing, structures in country towns around the state.

The soaring white sails of the Sydney Opera House were completed by 1967, but the design of the interior had still not been finalised. In circumstances that recalled Walter Burley Griffin's dispute with officialdom during the building of Canberra the Danish architect, Joern Utzon, had resigned from the project in 1966 after a long series of acrimonious exchanges with the Public Works Department. Utzon's original design had been revolutionary and experimental in character. Against his and the consulting engineers' better judgement work began on the building in 1959 before many important design and engineering problems had been properly resolved. The crux of the disputes was probably the seemingly uncontrollable rise in estimated costs, which were a severe embarrassment to the government and a cause of public resentment. After Utzon's departure a team of Australian architects designed the interior halls in a way that robbed the spectacular shells of any functional purpose and that, in the opinion of many, seriously compromised the integrity of the entire building.

During the 1950s and 1960s wool continued to be Australia's greatest export earner. Until the early sixties it accounted for almost half of Australia's total export earnings. For much of this period, too, Britain, the traditional destination for Australia's wool exports, continued to be the most important single customer, although its entry into the European Economic Community in the 1960s resulted in a significant drop in the British demand for Australian wool. Australia's wartime enemy, Japan, emerged during the 1950s as an increasingly important customer and by the mid-1960s had become the major buyer of Australian wool. Between 1950 and 1970 the number of sheep in Australia increased from 112 million to 180 million. This photograph shows sheep being mustered during the 1960s at Mern Merna in South Australia.

For ten years from 1958 large areas of Australia were ravaged by drought. Until 1966 the western, central and north-eastern parts of the continent were the worst affected, but from 1964 south-eastern Australia, including Tasmania, was hit. For Victoria, which had remained relatively unscathed until 1965, the worst years were 1967 and 1968. In this photograph the denuded paddocks of this normally rich agricultural area in East Gippsland demonstrate the extent of the destruction.

Drought, a tragically destructive force on its own, has many times in Australia been the trigger for another, more terrifying, destroyer — bushfire. On 7 February 1967 much of the south-east of Tasmania was ablaze as a result of blistering heat and fierce driving winds. At one stage the fires seemed likely to reach the centre of Hobart as flames roared down the slope of Mount Wellington. Sixty-two people died in the fires and eight townships were devastated. The worst affected was the small seaside town of Snug, about 30 kilometres from Hobart, where seven people died and more than 70 out of 123 houses, as well as the local carbide factory and the school, were destroyed. A number of people survived by rushing into the surf and staying there until the fire had subsided.

The 1960s saw the beginning of a mineral and mining boom in Australia and in particular the development of a lucrative iron-ore industry in the Pilbara region of Western Australia. In 1952 the pastoralist and industrialist Lang Hancock first discovered iron ore in the area while flying low over the Hamersley Ranges. Commercial exploitation did not begin, however, until a federal government ban on the export of iron ore was lifted in 1960. By 1965 7 million tonnes of iron ore had been produced and in 1966 the first major exports, mined by Hamersley Iron Ltd at Mount Tom Price, left the port of Dampier for Japan.

The top picture shows excavations taking place at Mount Tom Price for the construction of the railway to Dampier. In the bottom photograph Aborigines work on the 440-kilometre railway line that takes iron ore from the Mount Newman Joint Ventures' mine at Mount Whaleback to Port Hedland on the coast.

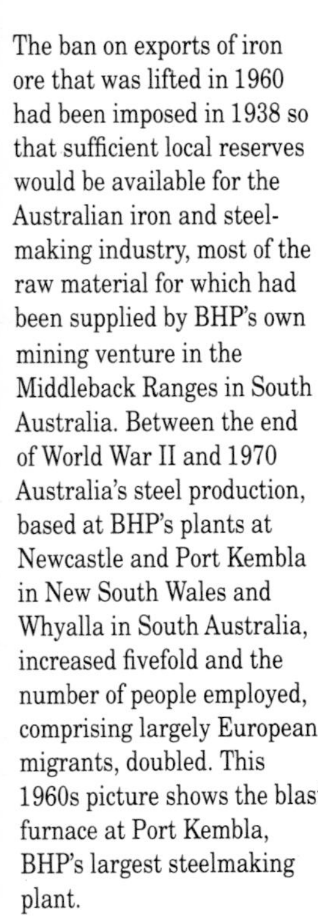

The ban on exports of iron ore that was lifted in 1960 had been imposed in 1938 so that sufficient local reserves would be available for the Australian iron and steel-making industry, most of the raw material for which had been supplied by BHP's own mining venture in the Middleback Ranges in South Australia. Between the end of World War II and 1970 Australia's steel production, based at BHP's plants at Newcastle and Port Kembla in New South Wales and Whyalla in South Australia, increased fivefold and the number of people employed, comprising largely European migrants, doubled. This 1960s picture shows the blast furnace at Port Kembla, BHP's largest steelmaking plant.

During the 1960s both onshore and offshore oilfields were discovered in Australia. In 1964 Australia's first commercial oilfield began production at Moonie in southern Queensland and the first offshore well was drilled off the coast of Gippsland in Victoria. The oil rig in this picture was operating in Bass Strait in the late 1960s.

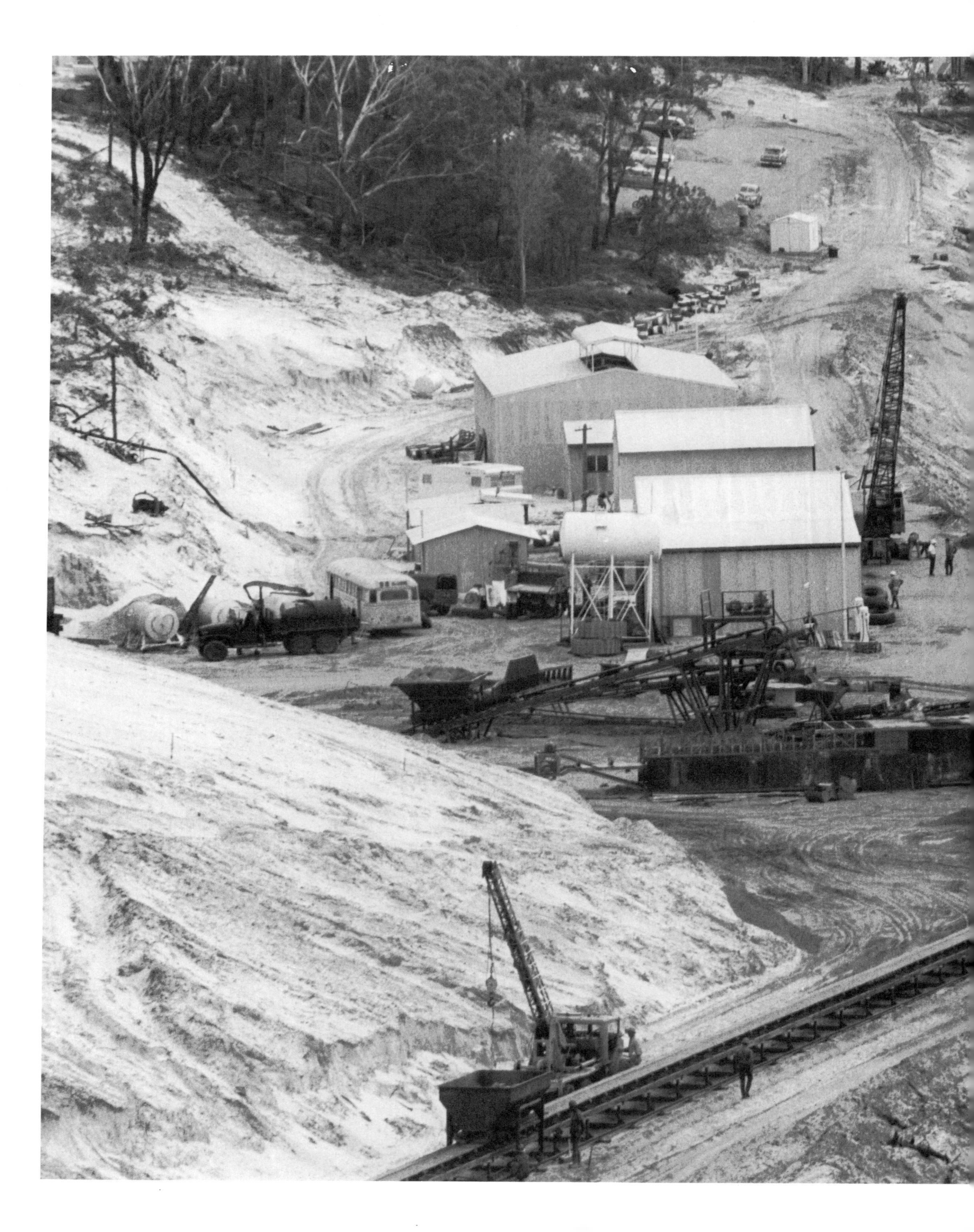

Mining sand for rutile and zircon on North Stradbroke Island off the Queensland coast in July 1966. Mining on the island, which had been the site of an Aboriginal reserve, began in 1950. Only in the 1970s did widespread concern about the environmental implications of sandmining begin to make itself felt.

8

Towards the Bicentenary

REMEMBER THE LAR
KULALUK. DARWIN N.
LAND RIGHTS CLAIMS
KULALUK FOR LARRAKIA 700 ACRES.
WE WUZ ROBBED
LAND BELONG TO WE. LARRAKIA
LAND RIGHTS NOW.
Perkins
Dexter

The early 1970s were for many Australians a time of almost exuberant optimism. There was a feeling abroad that new and more exciting times had arrived, that personal and national ideals could be striven for and attained and that Australia could achieve a stronger and more independent identity. A sometimes strident, but confident and positive militancy typified a number of 'movements' that took root and flourished during this period. The mood of the time, and the spirit of renewal it engendered, seemed to be epitomised in the ebullient figure of Gough Whitlam who, in December 1972, led Labor to power for the first time in 23 years, with the evocative slogan 'It's Time'. Labor, personified by Whitlam, was much better attuned to the reformist demands of the women's movement, the activists for Aboriginal land rights, the environmentalists, the proponents of homosexual law reform and to the interests of those advocating cultural renewal than were the conservative parties, which, squabbling among themselves and lacking strong leadership, gave the impression of being a spent force.

The exuberance was short-lived. Just three years after winning power Labor was ignominiously removed from office by the Governor-General, Sir John Kerr, who used his reserve powers — thought by many to be more token than real — to resolve a deadlock over the granting of supply. His action, which deeply alienated a large section of the community, was confirmed by the electorate, which accorded the conservative parties, under the aloof and dour Malcolm Fraser, a landslide victory.

Many of the reforms enacted by the Whitlam government were, however, maintained and even extended by the new regime, and Fraser surprised many of his bitterest opponents, and antagonised some of his more conservative colleagues, by his liberal stance on a number of issues.

Labor's declining fortunes resulted largely from a deteriorating international economic environment that was reflected in rising unemployment and falling business profits. Unemployment has remained high and the lack of job opportunities for young people continues to be a cause of great concern. In the late 1970s Australia's international debt began to grow and as the bicentenary approached had reached proportions that prompted some commentators to remind Australians anew of the lessons of the Great Depression.

The failure of a much-vaunted minerals boom to eventuate, the falling world prices for the commodities on which Australia has traditionally relied, and an inordinately high level of imports have caused Australians to look more critically at the assumptions that underlie the 'lucky country' mentality.

In 1983 another charismatic Labor leader, Robert Hawke, was elected to office. His pragmatic and cautious political style, however, has disconcerted many traditional Labor supporters, who had expected another government in the reformist Whitlam mould.

Previous pages: Sixty years after the opening of the first, and 'temporary', Parliament House, its successor, one of the most ambitious buildings ever undertaken in Australia, and built at a cost of about 1 billion dollars, nears completion. A hot air balloonist hovers over the site on Canberra's Capital Hill.

Left: In 1972 Aborigines demanding land rights for their people set up an 'Aboriginal Embassy' on the land opposite Parliament House.

On the death of Harold Holt in 1967 John Gorton was elected Leader of the Liberal Party and became Prime Minister in January 1968. Gorton's casual personal style, his unconventional social habits and his reputation as an enemy of states' rights quickly earned him the dislike of many conservatives. After losing ground in the 1969 elections he was challenged for the leadership. In March 1971, after the resignation of the Minister for Defence, Malcolm Fraser, who claimed that Gorton had been disloyal to him, he was replaced as Liberal Party Leader, and as Prime Minister, by William McMahon. This picture shows the deposed Gorton and the victorious McMahon descending the steps of Parliament House on 10 March 1971.

It has been claimed, unkindly, that McMahon would be remembered more for his glamorous wife, Sonia, than for any solid achievement as Prime Minister. Sonia certainly achieved international publicity with this photograph (*left*) of her and the Prime Minister attending a reception given for them in Washington by President Nixon.

Another leggy photograph (*right*), this time of the dynamic South Australian Labor Premier, Don Dunstan, and a young woman admirer. Dunstan, one of the most colourful politicians of the 1970s, became in 1970 the only Labor leader in Australia to hold office. His victory was seen by many as a precursor for a federal Labor victory. He remained Premier until his retirement, because of ill health, in 1979.

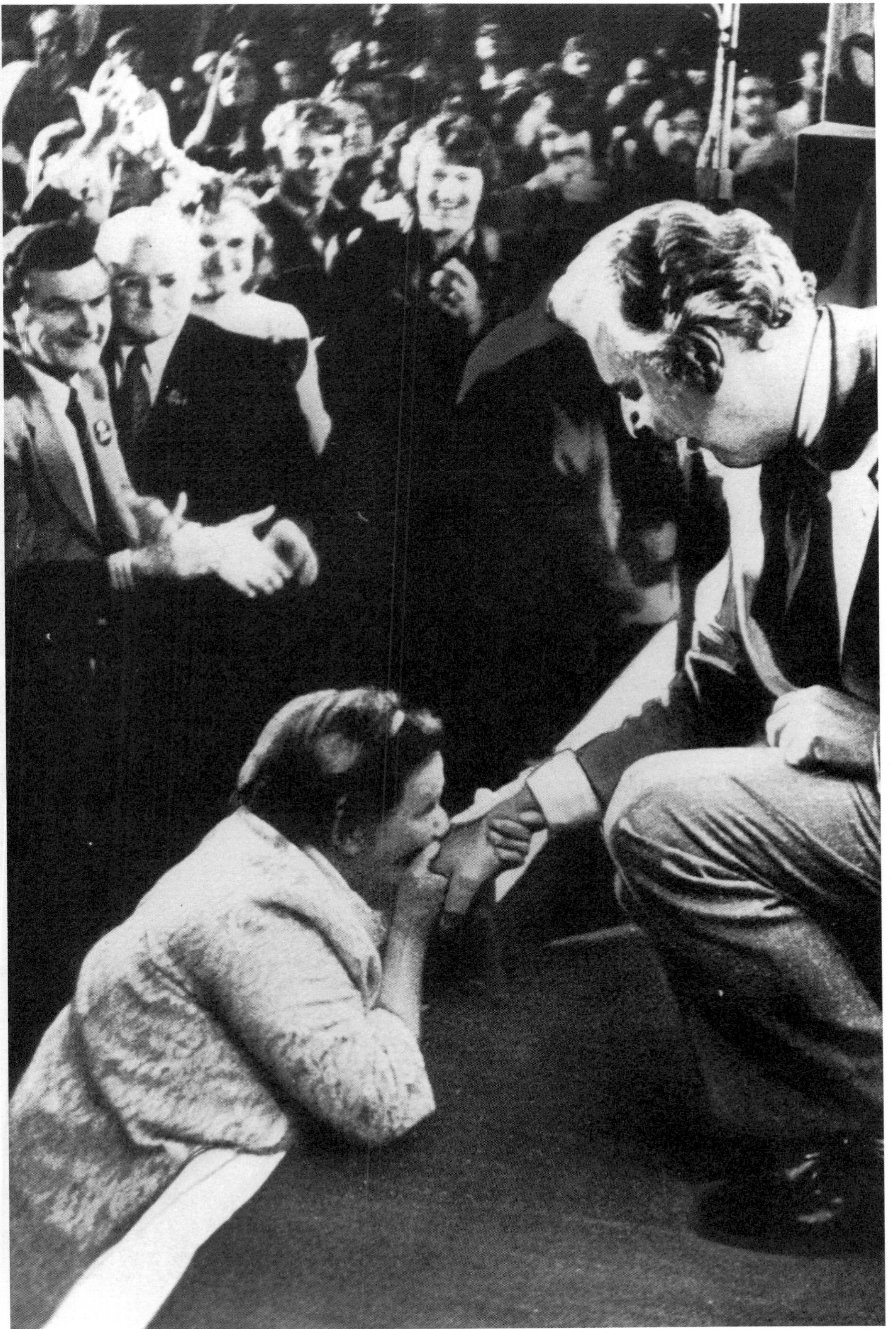

Labor came to power in the federal elections of December 1972 on the strength of Leader Gough Whitlam's personal popularity and on what was perceived to be the beginnings of an economic decline. Whitlam's image as a cultivated, articulate and visionary leader was enhanced by the comparatively lacklustre manner of his opponent, the Prime Minister, William McMahon, whom Whitlam tauntingly nicknamed 'Silly Billy'. The 1972 campaign ushered in the era of presidential-style electioneering in Australia. The opening of the Labor campaign was at a public, though expertly stage-managed and nationally televised, meeting in the outer western Sydney suburb of Blacktown. Whitlam entered to the strains of a band and the wild applause of the audience more like a conquering hero than one simply aspiring to power. His opening words, 'Men and women of Australia', were calculated to evoke memories of the wartime Labor Leader, Curtin, and the campaign slogan, 'It's time', looked back 23 years to a supposed golden age of Labor rule. At the end of his address this supporter rushed forward to kiss the future Prime Minister's hand. Among the euphoric onlookers is, at left, trade union leader Bob Hawke, who in 1983 would become the next Labor Prime Minister.

During its period in office the Labor government was plagued by a declining economy and, particularly towards the end, a series of scandals that culminated in an ill-advised and secretive attempt to borrow $4000 million using the services of an obscure broker, Tirath Khemlani. In October 1975 the Opposition, led by Malcolm Fraser, used its Senate majority to deny supply. After a prolonged impasse the Governor-General, Sir John Kerr, sacked Whitlam on 11 November and invited Fraser to head a caretaker government until elections could be held. In the top picture the Governor-General's secretary announces the termination of Whitlam's commission on the steps of Government House, while Whitlam, flushed with anger, waits to address the crowd. Minutes later Whitlam furiously denounced the Governor-General's actions and labelled Malcolm Fraser 'Kerr's cur'.

In the ensuing election, held on 13 December, the Labor Party was decisively defeated and Fraser was confirmed as Prime Minister. Fraser won another massive victory in 1977, a less comfortable one in 1980, and was defeated in 1983 by Labor under Bob Hawke. In the bottom picture the naturally shy and aloof Fraser uncharacteristically pours beers at an Italian workers' club in Brisbane.

During the 1975 election campaign Whitlam was buoyed by the huge crowds that turned out at his rallies and roared their support for his exhortation to 'maintain the rage'. At this rally, held in Sydney's Hyde Park on the day before the election, Whitlam shared the platform with Bob Hawke, who was president of both of the Australian Council of Trade Unions and of the Australian Labor Party. Even though he did not enter parliament until 1979, Hawke's Prime Ministerial ambitions were already a subject of wide speculation.

The hoarding in the background boldly proclaims Labor's campaign slogan, 'Shame, Fraser, Shame'. As a condemnation of what many saw as Fraser's cynical opportunism in denying supply and of his suspected collusion with the Governor-General, it was enthusiastically, and often loudly, taken up by Labor supporters.

This photograph of Sir Johannes Bjelke-Petersen with his wife and grandchildren epitomises the conservative values he has espoused and which have won him a record term — almost twenty years — as Premier of Queensland. A vociferous and fundamentalist Christian, he poses here after attending church to celebrate the return of his National Party government, with 39 per cent of the popular vote, in November 1986. In the early seventies Bjelke-Petersen was the scourge of the Whitlam government, whom he labelled dangerous socialists. He once defied established political convention by appointing an anti-Labor replacement for a deceased Labor senator. After his 1986 win Bjelke-Petersen, then in his 77th year, set his sights on the Prime Ministership, describing as 'inevitable' his ultimate accession to federal power.

During the 1970s and 1980s the plight of modern Aborigines has been highlighted by occasional outbursts of racial violence in country towns that have a significant Aboriginal population, and by an increased media interest in matters relating to Aboriginal health problems, living conditions and mortality rates. This photograph, taken in 1983 by Gerritt Fokkema, shows a prematurely aged Aboriginal woman standing in the doorway of her dilapidated house in the far western New South Wales town of Wilcannia, expressing in her look and posture the anguish of a life of deprivation.

285

Drought, one of the perennial scourges of the Australian countryside, affected large areas of Australia between 1976 and 1983. Although the worst period began in 1979, the dry Queensland summer of 1977-78 resulted in widespread stock losses and produced distressing scenes like this one, photographed on a property in the Kilcoy area.

City dwellers seldom have to confront directly many of the problems that affect people on the land. The long drought that had ravaged vast areas of the countryside was, however, forced dramatically on the attention of Melburnians when, in February 1983, a huge cloud of dust from normally lush dairy country descended on the city and suburbs.

In November 1970 Pope Paul VI, Supreme Pontiff of the Roman Catholic Church, visited Sydney as part of the Captain Cook bicentenary celebrations. During his visit the 73-year-old Pope celebrated a 'bicentenary mass' at Randwick Racecourse and recited the Lord's Prayer at an ecumenical service in the Sydney Town Hall. The visit demonstrated the extent to which age-old enmities between Catholics and Protestants had been broken down, as well as the more prominently political profile the papacy had assumed. In this photograph the Pope symbolically embraces the crowd as he arrives at Randwick racecourse for the mass.

In November 1986 another Pope, the Polish-born John Paul II, toured Australia and received the kind of welcome that in earlier times was reserved for members of the royal family. His visit excited not only members of his own church, but also people who had little sympathy with the tenets of that church. Even those who disliked his inflexible attitude to matters of sexual morality and the role of women in the church were impressed by the style of the man. His tour vividly indicated the enhanced role of the papacy in world affairs and as a perceived force for world peace. At the end of a youth rally at the Sydney Cricket Ground the Pope, in a gesture that would have been unthinkable for almost any former pontiff, joined hands and danced with these young people.

In Australia Church leaders have generally welcomed the gains made by women in their quest for equality of opportunity in other areas, but most have strongly resisted any pretensions to equality within the Church itself. The campaign for the admission of women to the ministry and priesthood, however, has persisted and has won some significant gains. While the Catholic Church remains officially adamant on the issue, there are signs that the Anglicans, although bitterly split on the matter, are yielding ground. The Reverend Marjorie McGregor, a deacon of the Anglican Church, has her own parish in Melbourne, but as yet cannot be admitted to the full priesthood. She was one of eighteen women ordained in Victoria during 1986.

Although the gay liberation movement won the sympathetic support of many Christians, the churches generally regarded it with disfavour. Despite a climate of growing public tolerance there have been numerous attempts to have known homosexuals barred or removed from positions of influence and responsibility. This demonstration was against the sacking of a homosexual Anglican Church official in a Sydney parish in 1972.

The women's liberation movement was one of the most important campaigns of the 1970s and had significant and lasting ramifications. It was often perceived and depicted in the popular media either as being manipulated by a small and vociferous group of dangerous radicals, dedicated to the overthrow of the social order, or as an amusing, if sometimes irritating, and temporary social aberration. If, however, some of its manifestations were shrill and aggressive, the women's movement was a complex phenomenon, concerned with a wide range of issues that were promoted with great intellectual force and clarity. While perhaps the most publicised issue was the highly emotive and divisive one of the right to abortion — being loudly demanded (*top*) in this march in Melbourne in 1974 — the movement was equally concerned with matters such as childcare, equality of employment opportunities, wage justice and the financial and sexual exploitation of women. Men and women often cooperated in their campaigns for reform, as in the demonstration (*bottom left*) for the provision of childcare facilities. A reform that resulted from the women's movement was the admission of women into jobs that had formerly been considered 'unfeminine'. The photograph (*bottom right*) shows girls training to be welders and mechanics.

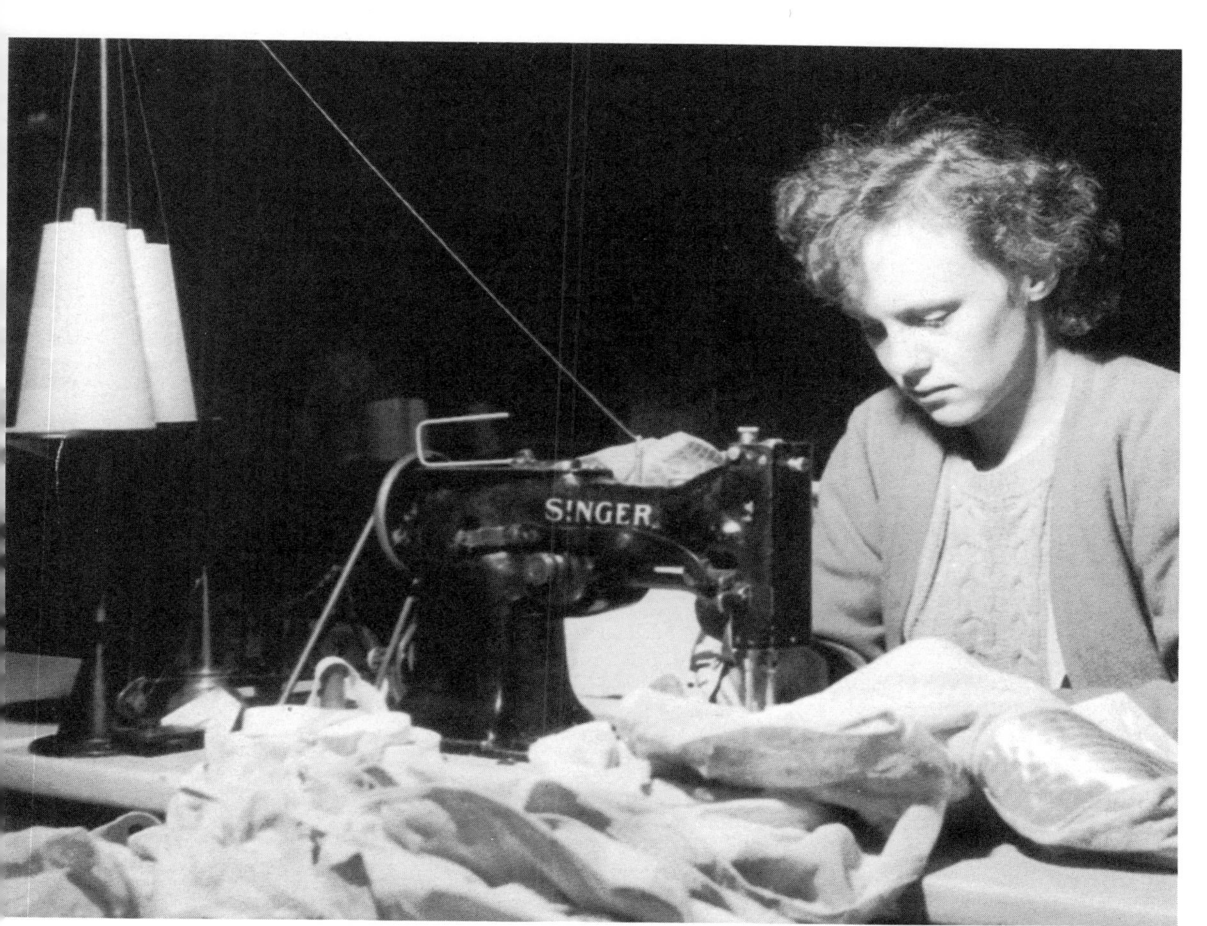

An example of financial exploitation is the use of 'outworkers', who work for very low rates of pay on their own premises and with their own equipment, mainly in the clothing industry. Being self-employed they are paid only for work completed and are not covered by any awards or protected by insurance or compensation. Most of them are migrant women.

Nurses, who had often been pressured into not taking militant action against poor conditions and wages by cynical appeals to their 'dedication', began taking to the streets in their quest for wage justice.

Within a period of two weeks in the summer of 1974-75, two major disasters occurred — one, the work of a natural force, occurred in the tropical north of the continent; the other, the result of human misadventure, happened almost at the southern extreme. On Christmas Day 1974, Cyclone Tracy devastated Darwin, and on the night of 5 January 1975 a 11 000-tonne ore freighter, the *Lake Illawarra*, hit two piers of Hobart's eleven-year-old Tasman Bridge, bringing down part of the roadway and sending four cars hurtling into the Derwent River. The ship sank with the loss of six crew members; five motorists and passengers perished.

On 18 January 1977 another bridge was involved in an accident. This aerial photograph conveys some idea of the carnage that resulted when an electric train travelling during the morning peak hour from the Blue Mountains to Sydney came off the rails and hit a support of an overhead rail bridge. The bridge collapsed on top of a section of the train, killing 83 people and severely injuring many others. It was the worst train disaster ever in Australia.

This was the scene that greeted shocked residents of Darwin when they emerged from wherever they had managed to shelter during the dark early hours of Christmas Day 1974 while Cyclone Tracy worked out its destructive fury. Many buildings simply collapsed before the force of the 217-kilometre-per-hour winds and it is difficult to believe that the total death toll was not more than fifty. Even though Darwin had been hit twice before — in 1897 and 1937 — by cyclones, and was in a region subject to cyclone activity, most of its buildings were not constructed to withstand the impact of high winds.

Less than a year earlier, during the Australia Day weekend in January 1974, the aftermath of another cyclone, Cyclone Wanda, had caused Brisbane to be invaded by floodwaters. The picture on the left shows some of the 7000 homes that were completely or partially submerged. On 28 January the floods entered the centre of the city. This boy (*right*) is wading waist deep at the corner of Margaret and Albert Streets.

The communist victory in Vietnam in 1974 effectively put the final nail into the coffin of the 'White Australia' policy. Attitudes towards Asian immigration had begun to change during the 1950s when large numbers of young Asians came to study in Australia under the Colombo Plan, but there was no large-scale Asian immigration to Australia until the mid-1970s. From 1975 hundreds of thousands of South Vietnamese, dispossessed by the new regime, set sail in all manner of craft from Vietnam. Many of them perished at sea, but most managed to reach other parts of Asia where they were accommodated, sometimes begrudgingly, in transit camps. The picture at top left shows refugees escaping from a sinking boat off the coast of Malaysia. Most countries, including Australia, were reluctant to accept them. Some set out again by boat and from late 1977 a steady stream of 'boat people', uninvited and largely unwelcomed, began arriving on Australia's northern coast. The boat shown at top right arrived in Darwin in 1978. The boat people virtually forced the government to accept a reasonable intake of refugees and by 1983 over 70 000 Vietnamese refugees had settled in Australia. The man in the centre picture, being reunited with his family at Melbourne airport in 1982, was one of the first people to come to Australia with the agreement of the Vietnamese government.

The young Vietnamese woman (*bottom left*) is learning English at a migrant centre in Melbourne. The two boys (*bottom right*) at a fun park in Sydney look thoroughly at home.

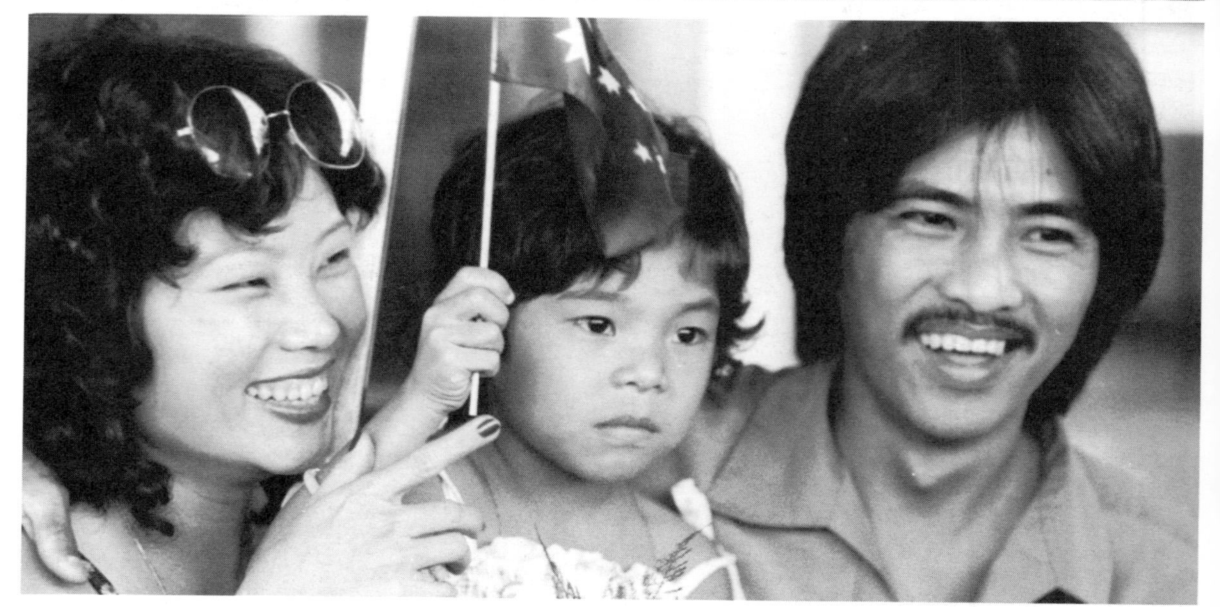

The notion that migrants to Australia should become assimilated into the predominantly Anglo-Saxon culture gave way during the 1970s to the concept of 'multiculturalism', which took heed of the fact that almost all migrants, like the two Yugoslav women in the top photograph, maintained aspects of their cultural traditions and often continued to speak their native languages and to bring up their children to be bilingual. The ideal of a monocultural society was replaced by one of harmonious diversity in which groups would be encouraged to maintain and nurture their separate cultural identities. These ideas were behind the setting-up, under government sponsorship, of multicultural television and radio stations. The Melbourne and Sydney television stations broadcast subtitled programs in a variety of languages. They adopted the slogan 'A whole world of people', which is exemplified in the publicity shot at bottom left.

The man (*bottom right*) on the beach at Surfers Paradise, on Queensland's Gold Coast, is one of the many tourists from Japan and other parts of Asia who have found Australia a congenial and relatively inexpensive holiday destination.

In 1986 Gough Whitlam, in the National Gallery in Canberra, poses in front of the painting that caused such a furore when his government purchased it in 1973 for $1.3 million — *Blue Poles* by the American painter Jackson Pollock. With the painting now generally acknowledged as a classic of its genre, and with its value confirmed as greatly in excess of its purchase price, the decision to invest in it can be considered to have been vindicated on artistic as well as economic grounds. At the time of its acquisition, Pollock's painting, like many of the artistic ventures that gained government support, evoked a knee-jerk philistine reaction.

The despoliation of the environment by developers, miners, industrial complexes as well as by the average litterbugging citizen became a matter of national concern during the 1970s. A number of media campaigns were launched to make people aware of their environmental responsibilities. In this photograph the popular television personality Norman Gunston (alias Gary McDonald) looks askance at an assortment of debris that has been dumped in the Yarra.

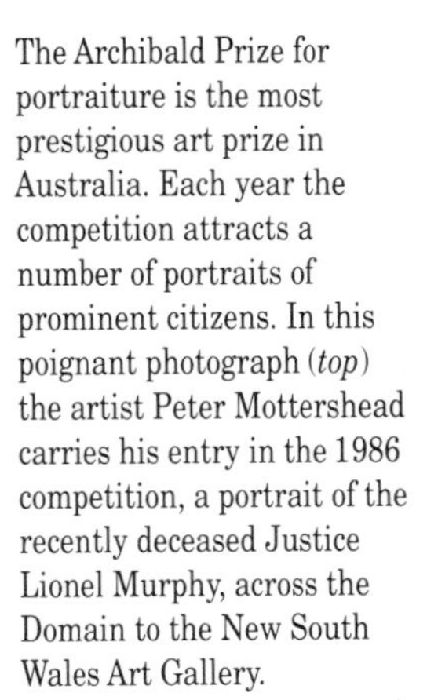

The Archibald Prize for portraiture is the most prestigious art prize in Australia. Each year the competition attracts a number of portraits of prominent citizens. In this poignant photograph (*top*) the artist Peter Mottershead carries his entry in the 1986 competition, a portrait of the recently deceased Justice Lionel Murphy, across the Domain to the New South Wales Art Gallery.

Lionel Murphy was one of the most prominent public figures of the seventies and eighties. He was a reformist Attorney-General in the Whitlam government and the architect of the 1975 Family Law Act, which rationalised and simplified divorce law in Australia. To the dismay of many conservatives he was appointed to the High Court, where he distinguished himself by his lucid and succinct judgments on a number of controversial issues. During the 1980s he became the centre of controversy when he was charged with 'conspiracy to pervert the course of justice' on the strength of some illegally taped phone conversations, in which he was alleged to have sought favoured treatment for a former associate who was charged with a criminal offence. Murphy was found guilty and then, on appeal, not guilty. Soon after the vindicating verdict, it was revealed that Murphy was suffering from terminal cancer, from which he died in late 1986. This photograph (*bottom*) of Murphy and his wife, Ingrid, vividly shows the anguish that the public ordeal had subjected them to.

The famous maxi yacht *Apollo V (top left)*, veteran of a number of Sydney to Hobart races, owned by West Australian millionaire Alan Bond, is seen here in the 1981 race. Probably more than any other event the highly publicised annual Sydney to Hobart race ensured that sailing maintained a high public profile. When, however, an Australian syndicate, under the leadership of Alan Bond, succeeded in wresting the America's Cup from the New York Yacht Club in 1983 with his yacht *Australia II (top right)*, the national enthusiasm verged on hysteria. In the bottom photograph Bond and his wife acknowledge the acclamation of the crowds as they travel in a triumphant motorcade through Perth on their return to Australia after *Australia II*'s historic victory. In the 1987 challenge, which took place off Fremantle, the cup returned to the United States when the Australian defender, *Kookaburra II*, was comprehensively outclassed by the American challenger.

The recession of the mid-1970s brought a high level of unemployment to Australia that, despite sporadic improvements, persisted throughout the 1980s. The group hardest hit was young people, and youth unemployment has been the most serious social problem in Australia's recent history. Demonstrations like this one, in which young people in Collins Street, Melbourne, publicly assert their right to work, have become commonplace throughout Australia in recent years.

The economic hard times that have resulted in unremittingly high levels of unemployment have produced homelessness on a scale unknown in Australia since the days of the Great Depression. High interest rates have spelt the end of the 'great Australian dream' of home ownership, and a consequent acute shortage of rental accommodation, coupled with the inability of many to pay high rents, has forced an increasing number of people onto the streets or, in the case of these three young people, into the parks. They are sleeping under the palms in Brisbane's Botanic Gardens.

A new and invaluable addition was made to Sydney's, and Australia's, cultural heritage when the Sydney Opera House was opened by Queen Elizabeth II on 20 October 1973. The enormous cost of 110 million dollars; the intense bitterness that had been generated; the frustrations and tensions that had resulted from constant delays; the continuing feeling of betrayal that had caused Joern Utzon, the creative force behind the whole project, to stay away from the opening; none of these marred the splendour of the occasion. During the day thousands had crowded onto small and large boats and taken to the water to get a better view of proceedings; in the evening fireworks exploded in the darkness, throwing into spectacular relief the the gleaming sail-like shells.

In the early hours of Saturday 21 April 1979 about 700 people stood in impotent protest as bulldozers brutally reduced to rubble another part of Australia's cultural heritage — Brisbane's once beautiful and almost century-old Bellevue Hotel. Like similarly valuable buildings in other Australian cities the Bellevue, shown (*top*) in 1973 before it had been allowed to fall into dilapidated disrepair, was making way for the insatiable demands of high-rise developers. The demolition, carried out under heavy police protection, was executed in the dead of night in order to minimise possible obstruction from protesters.

Acknowledgements

We are grateful for permission to reproduce photographs and we would like to thank the following: Adelaide State Library, SA, p. 196 (bottom); *The Age*, Melbourne, pp. 162, 195, 242 (top right), 266 (top), 269 (bottom), 286 (top), 291 (top), 294 (centre), 295 (top), 296 (bottom right); Archives Authority of NSW, Sydney, p. 78 (bottom right); Arnotts Pty Ltd, Sydney, p. 134 (bottom); AUSTCARE, UNHCR/15057/P, Sydney, p.294 (top left); Australian Broadcasting Corporation, Sydney, p. 251 (bottom left); Australian Bureau & News Information, Sydney, pp. 233 (bottom), 276, 293 (top); Australian Consolidated Press, Sydney, pp. 177 (top right), 212, 247 (top); Australian Institute of Aboriginal Studies, Canberra, p. 194 photo no. N1599.28; Australian National Gallery, Canberra, p. 159 Harold Cazneaux — 'The Old and the New' © 1929; Australian Railway Historical Society, Melbourne, p. 31 (bottom); Australian War Memorial, Canberra, pp. 84 & 85 photo no. E1187, 86 photo no. H11568, 88 (bottom) photo no. A3404, 89 photo no. H11609, 90 (top) photo no. J3241, 90 (bottom) photo no. EN500, 91 photo no. A3414, 92 (top) photo no. EN194, 92 (bottom) photo no. G1442A, 93 photo no. H11583, 94 (bottom left) photo no. A1854, 94 (bottom right) photo no.G1812, 95 (top) photo no. A879, 95 (centre) photo no.G408, 95 (bottom) photo no. G1440A, 96 (top) photo no. G1810C, 96 (bottom left) photo no. J6392, 96 (bottom right) photo no. A2025, 97 photo no. G1126, 98 & 99 photo no. H2386, 100 (bottom left) photo no. H17373, 100 (bottom right) photo no. H12155, 102 (top) photo no. B1507, 102 (bottom) photo no. B1627, 103 (top) photo no. B10, 103 (bottom) photo no. B78, 104 (top) photo no. C4337, 104 (bottom) photo no. C2305, 105 (top) photo no. J346, 105 (bottom left) photo no. J360, 106 photo no. H11572, 107 (top) photo no. H11613, 107 (bottom) photo no. H3376, 108 (bottom) photo no. H11604, 109 photo no. H11585, 112 (top) photo no. EZ3, 112 (bottom left) photo no. E2649, 112 (bottom right) photo no. H16101, 113 (top) photo no. EL110, 113 (bottom) photo no. E51, 114 & 115 photo no. E7111, 116 (top) photo no. E732, 116 (bottom left) photo no. E4677, 116 (bottom right) photo no. E2371, 117 (top) photo no. E1400, 117 (centre) photo no. K114, 117 (bottom) photo no. E3648, 118 (top) photo no. D421, 118 (centre) photo no. E2655, 118 (bottom) photo no. E3046, 120 (top) photo no. H11576, 120 (bottom) photo no. H18785, 198 & 199 photo no. 304/1, 202 (bottom) photo no. 2837/17, 206 (bottom) photo no. 42202, 207 (top) photo no. 20792, 207 (bottom) photo no. 20279, 208 (bottom) photo no. 26499, 214 (bottom) photo no. 136390, 216 (bottom) photo no. 12422, 218 (top) photo no. 15714, 218 (bottom left) photo no. 26821, 218 (bottom right) photo no. 14028, 219 (top) photo no. 14082, 221 (bottom right) photo no. 44516, 223 (top) photo no. 11538, 223 (bottom) photo no. 141413, 226 (top) photo no. 136413, 227 (top) photo no. 141960, 227 (centre) photo no. 140313, 227 (bottom left) photo no. 42773, 227 (bottom right) photo no. 136997, 228 (top) photo no. 28614, 229 (bottom) photo no. 19199, 230 (top) photo no. 110436, 230 (bottom) photo no. 19296, 240; Barrie Bell Photographer, GTV9 Sydney, pp. 250, 251 (top); Courtesy Battye Library, Western Australia, 25 (top), 152 (bottom); BBC Hulton Picture Library, London, p. 94 (top); COO-EE Historical Picture Library, Melbourne, p. 27 (top); *The Courier-Mail*, Brisbane, p. 293 (bottom left); Dept. of Agriculture, Victoria, pp.132 (bottom), 154 & 155; John Fairfax & Sons Pty Ltd, Sydney, pp. 111 (bottom), 168 (top), 176 (top), 177 (top left), 186, 206 (top), 214 (top), 215 (bottom left), 216 (top), 200, 220, 221 (top), 221 (bottom left), 222 (top), 224 (bottom), 231 (top), 231 (bottom), 232 (top), 234 (bottom), 246, 256 (bottom), 274 & 275, 282, 283, 288 (bottom), 289 (top), 290 (bottom right), 291 (bottom),

297 (top), 297 (bottom); General Motors Holden, Melbourne, p. 233 (top); Hartland & Hyde Activities Pty Ltd, Sydney, p. 265; Herald & Weekly Times Limited, Melbourne, pp. 133 (top), 140, 142 (bottom), 142 (top), 147 (top), 148 (top), 153 (centre), 158, 164 (top), 165, 172 (top), 172 (bottom), 174 (left), 175 (top), 175 (bottom), 179 (top), 182 (bottom), 183 (bottom), 183 (top), 184 (top), 185 (left), 185 (top right), 185 (bottom), 194 (bottom left), 194 (bottom right), 204, 208 (top), 213, 232 (bottom), 245 (bottom left), 245 (bottom right), 247 (bottom right), 248 (bottom left), 252, 254, 256 (top left), 261 (bottom right), 271 (bottom), 290 (top), 294 (top right), 298 (top); Fred Lang, Gold Coast, Queensland, pp. 186 & 187, 255 (bottom); *The Mercury*, Hobart, p. 292 (top); Metropolitan Water, Sewerage & Drainage Board, Sydney, p. 264 (bottom right); Mildenhall Collection, Sydney, p. 135 (bottom); *The Mirror*, Sydney, p. 257; National Library of Australia, Canberra, pp. 15 (bottom, 16 (bottom) William Henry Corkhill, Tilba Tilba Collection, 17, 18 (bottom), 28 (bottom), 58 (top), 41 (top), 44, 50 (top) Nan Kyvell Collection, 52 (bottom), 53 (bottom), 58 (top), 80 (bottom), 80 (top), 81 (top), 83 (bottom) William Henry Corkhill, Tilba Tilba Collection, 101 (bottom) Cazneaux Collection, 111 (top), 121 (top) Cazneaux Collection, 128 & 129, 130, 132 (top), 135 (top), 136 & 137, 139 (bottom left), 139 (bottom right), 141, 145 (bottom), 146 (top), 147 (bottom), 159 Cazneaux Collection, 192 (top), 236 & 237, 243 (bottom right), 280 (bottom); New England Historical Resource Centre, Armadale CAE, Armadale, p. 105 (bottom right); News Ltd, Sydney, pp. 177 (bottom), 241 (bottom), 247 (bottom left), 251 (bottom right), 253 (bottom), 255 (top), 256 (top right), 261 (bottom left), 269 (top), 278 (top), 278 (bottom left), 280 (top), 298 (bottom), 290 (bottom left), 292, 294 (bottom right), 300; NSW Department of Education, Sydney, pp. 76 (top), 101 (top), 131 (top); NSW Government Printer, Sydney, pp. 31 (top), 35 (bottom), 40 (top), 40 (bottom), 42 (top), 46 & 47, 50 (bottom), 51, 54 & 55, 59 (top), 60 & 61, 70 (top), 72, 73 (top), 73 (bottom), 76 (bottom), 75 (bottom right), 78 (top), 126, 127 (centre), 127 (bottom), 134 (top) photo no. 13960, 169 (right); NSW Housing Commission, Sydney, pp. 262 (top), 262 (bottom); Nicholas Kiwi Pty Ltd, Melbourne, p. 245 (top); Northern Regional Library, Launceston, dust jacket, p. 2; Peter O'Halloran, Brisbane, p. 299 (bottom); Collection: John Oxley Library, Brisbane, pp. 65, 69, 138, 139 (top), 144, 157 (top); David Parker, Melbourne, p. 266 (bottom); Dept. of Primary Industries, Brisbane, pp. 284 & 285; Public Library, South Australia, pp. 75 (bottom) P. J. Noye Collection, 77 P. J. Noye Collection; QANTAS, Melbourne, p. 193 (top); Queensland Newspapers, Brisbane, pp. 293 (bottom right), 301 (top), 301 (bottom); Royal Historical Society of Victoria, Melbourne, pp. 27 (bottom left), 32 & 33, 53 (top); Science Museum of Victoria, Melbourne, p. 19; Special Broadcasting Service, Sydney, p. 295; South Australian Archives, Adelaide, p. 25 (bottom); State Library of NSW (Mitchell Library), Sydney, pp. 2 (top), 20 (top) Holtermann Collection, p. 21 (bottom) Holtermann Collection, 68 (top), 83 (top), 110, 124, 153 (bottom), 168 (bottom right), 255 (bottom); State Library of South Australia, Adelaide, pp. 36 (top), 42 (bottom), 59 (bottom), 63 (top), 64 (top), 64 (bottom), 68 (bottom), 69 (top), 127 (top), 145 (top), 152 (top), 181, 182 (top), 215 (top); State Library of Victoria (La Trobe), Melbourne, pp. 15 (top), 16 (top), 22 (bottom), 37 (bottom), 41 (bottom), 229 (top); Mark Strizic, Melbourne, p. 264 (top left); Stuart Penberthy Pty Ltd, Photographers, Melbourne, p. 263 (bottom); *Sydney Morning Herald*, Sydney, pp. 234 (top), 248 (top), 249, 260 (top), 253 (top), 295 (bottom right); Telecom Australia, Melbourne, pp. 34 (top), 35 (top), 143 (bottom), 192 (bottom); *Tribune*, Sydney, p. 261 (top); Victorian Historical Society, Melbourne, p. 23; Victorian Soil Conservation Authority, Victoria, p. 133 (bottom); V-Line Photographics, Melbourne, pp. 240 (bottom), 241 (top), 242 (bottom); Weldon Trannies, McMahon's Point, South Australia, pp. 108 (top), 143, 168 (bottom left), 173 (top), 173 (bottom), 193 (bottom), 197 (top), 205, 217, 222 (bottom), 243 (top), 281; West Australian Newspapers Limited, Perth, pp. 36 (bottom), 179 (bottom), 298 (bottom).

While every effort has been made to trace and acknowledge copyright, in some cases copyright proved untraceable. Should any infringement have occurred, the publishers tender their apologies.

BLADEN COUNTY PUBLIC LIBRARY
T 30594